UNITED NATIONS ECONOMIC COMMISSION

**NATIONAL INSTITUTES
OF HEALTH**

**NATIONAL INSTITUTE
ON AGING**

AGEING RESEARCH IN EUROPE:
DEMOGRAPHIC, SOCIAL AND
BEHAVIOURAL ASPECTS

Written by

Emily M. Agree
Department of Population Dynamics
School of Hygiene and Public Health
Johns Hopkins University

and

George C. Myers
Center for Demographic Studies
Duke University

UNITED NATIONS

New York and Geneva, 1998

EXPLANATORY NOTES

The designations employed and the presentation of the material in this publication do not imply the expression of any opinion whatsoever on the part of the Secretariat of the United Nations concerning the legal status of any country, territory, city or area, or of its authorities, or concerning the delimitation of its frontiers or boundaries.

The views expressed herein are those of the individual authors and do not necessarily reflect the views of the United Nations nor the institutions with which the authors are affiliated.

The following symbols have been used throughout this paper:

A dash (-) indicates nil or negligible.
Two dots (..) indicates not available or not pertinent.

The following abbreviations have been used:

DHHS	Department of Health and Human Services
NIA	National Institute on Aging
NIH	National Institutes of Health
UN/ECE	United Nations Economic Commission for Europe
UNFPA	United Nations Population Fund

UNITED NATIONS PUBLICATION

Sales No. GV.E.98.0.1

ISBN 92-1-100762-3
ISSN 1014-4994

Acknowledgements

The Population Activities Unit of the United Nations Economic Commission for Europe and the authors would like to thank the many individuals who contributed to this survey of population ageing-related research. In particular, we would like to express our appreciation to Mitchell Eggers, who designed and supervised the fielding of the ECE ageing surveys, Mattie Dijkstra for her assistance in distributing and processing the initial results of the survey; and Jelena Torbica and Peter D. Myers for editing and respectively preparing the Wave 1 and 2 databases, respectively, from the original questionnaires, as well as Phillipe Chauvet for his general assistance with the work on the survey. The efforts of all of the principal investigators, project managers, administrators, and researchers who gave generously of their time to complete the questionnaires and assist with this survey are also gratefully acknowledged.

PREFACE

The member states of the United Nations Economic Commission for Europe (UN/ECE) are experiencing demographic changes which are posing unique public policy challenges. Population ageing, one of the most salient long-term developments in the region, has been under way for several decades, although the timing and pace of the fundamental shifts in population age structures vary across countries and sub-regions. The increasing importance of this phenomenon is reflected in the attention paid to the opportunities and challenges of ageing populations at the 1997 Denver Summit of the leading industrialized nations. Various other international and national forums have also emphasized the concern of both governments and the broader public about the consequences of population ageing and the social and economic status of older people. The differences in demographic history and in current social, economic, and political realities create different priorities across countries and have implications on research and policy action. Nevertheless, there is now a common understanding of the need to address the issues of population ageing through a coherent system of policy measures that are based on sound research of the social and economic consequences of this process. In recognition of this, the United Nations has designated 1999 as the International Year of Older Persons and has developed several international instruments on ageing, including the International Plan of Action on Ageing, the United Nations Principles for Older Persons and the United Nations Targets on Ageing for the Year 2001.

In an effort to further help national governments and non-governmental organizations meet the challenges posed by population ageing, the UN/ECE, with the financial support of the United Nations Population Fund (UNFPA), has been active for years in addressing this issue. Its work on population ageing is guided, among other things, by the understanding that older persons make social and economic contributions, thus population ageing should be considered as an opportunity rather than a burden for society; that they are a heterogeneous group, with a diversity resulting from differences in gender, socio-economic conditions, health status and cultural background, and that this requires clearly defined, multi-faceted and well-targeted policy instruments and responses. Also recognizing the urgent need for better information and data collection on which to base well-informed and effective policy-making, the UN/ECE has been coordinating various data-collection and research activities in the field of population ageing. These include several successive projects carried out by the UN/ECE's Population Activities Unit (PAU), which resulted in, among other things, the collection of a unique set of census-based microdata samples, that is currently being used to study the social and economic conditions of older persons. This work has been carried out by the PAU in collaboration with the Office of Demography at the United States National Institute on Aging (NIA) and with co-funding from the UNFPA. The NIA, one of the Institutes at the National Institutes of Health (NIH), leads the United States' efforts on ageing research.

This report is another outcome of the UN/ECE's work in the field of population ageing. It summarizes the major findings of a survey on ageing-related research in Europe carried out by the PAU in collaboration with the NIA. The goals of the survey were to take stock of population ageing-related research in the European countries, to identify innovative data collection and research strategies and high-quality survey instruments that can be used throughout the region in future data collection and research efforts, and to find out what type of cross-national ageing research should be initiated in Europe during the coming years. The survey was carried out in two waves. The first wave covered over 300 projects from about 150 institutions and individuals. The results of this wave will be published simultaneously with this report in a compendium entitled *Directory of Population Ageing-Related Research Projects in Europe.* The second wave collected additional, detailed information for around 50 of the original wave one projects, most of which are large-scale, nationally representative research efforts involving primary data collection. That information is analyzed in the current report which complements the *Directory.*

The report highlights the conceptual and methodological developments and achievements in the ageing-related research being conducted in Europe in the 1990s. Its overall conclusion, however, is that much of the social and bio-medical research in the field has been problem-driven rather than theory-driven and is still mostly descriptive rather than analytical. The report also identifies important gaps in both the available data sources and in our understanding of the consequences of population ageing. As the authors point out, although many excellent longitudinal studies are being undertaken, they remain limited in geographic scope and substantive complexity, which make them ill-suited to address broad policy questions such as those related to health and health care financing, or social security and pension schemes. Filling these gaps requires concerted international efforts in the research and data collection spheres, and closer collaboration between national and international institutions and researchers across the region. The UN/ECE hopes that the publication of the *Research on Ageing in Europe* report and its companion *Directory* will enhance networking opportunities and thus facilitate future international collaborative efforts in addressing this important issue.

Yves Berthelot
Executive Secretary
United Nations Economic Commission for Europe

Richard J. Hodes
Director
National Institute on Aging

TABLE OF CONTENTS

1 INTRODUCTION

The member states of the ECE have been particularly concerned with the social and economic consequences of population ageing. All of the European and North American nations are experiencing population ageing, although the timing and pace of age structure transitions varies across countries and regions. Some countries, such as France and Sweden, began the process of population ageing by the middle of the last century, while others have experienced increases in the relative size of their aged populations only during the past few decades. Such differences in demographic history create different priorities across countries. Additionally, distinctions in social, economic, and political realities in each country mean that the focal areas of research and policy show considerable diversity.

The Population Activities Unit, with support from the United States National Institute on Aging (NIA) and the United Nations Fund for Population Activities (UNFPA), has undertaken to document major research efforts in the ageing field across the European continent. The goals of the project were threefold: first, to take stock of ageing research in Europe; second, to identify innovative research strategies and high-quality survey instruments that might be used in future ageing research; and third, to suggest strategies for cross-national research that might be initiated in Europe during the coming five to seven years. In order to accomplish these goals, an institutional survey was designed to collect information on research projects, funding institutions, data collection efforts, and the availability of quantitative data on the health, economic, and social consequences of population ageing. The project also solicited views from experts across the region on desirable directions for future research on ageing in Europe.

The survey was conducted in two waves. The first wave collected baseline information on a wide range of projects (over 300 in all) and the results are reported in: *The Directory of Ageing Research in Europe*. The second wave of the survey, which provides the basis of this report, provides more detailed information on population-based research projects in the demographic, social, and economic aspects of ageing.

This is the first time that a comprehensive cataloguing of ageing research projects has been undertaken for the ECE European member nations. The authors recognise that some relevant projects may not have been identified in the initial data collection phase. Moreover, it was not possible to collect detailed information from all research efforts involved in the study of ageing. Instead, it was necessary to focus on a specific set of issues of importance in looking at the overall impact of recent demographic changes on the economic and social well-being of citizens in the member states. We trust that this survey may be viewed as a first step in the process of communication among researchers and policymakers in Europe, and that it will lead to further integration and sharing of knowledge across institutional and political boundaries.

1.1 Scope of the Report

This report is based primarily on the findings of a survey of recent, on-going, and planned ageing-related research in Europe carried out in 1995 and 1996 by the Population Activities Unit of the UN/ECE. Topics covered in the survey are relatively wide in scope with most major subject areas of ageing-related research included. The design and organisation of the survey itself is described in more detail in Section 3. This report also focuses on the medium to large scale population-based research projects dealing with demographic, social, economic, health and epidemiological aspects of ageing that were surveyed in the second wave of data collection.

1.2 Structure of the Report

The introductory section of the report describes the goals of the PAU survey on ageing research in Europe, and the scope and organisation of this report. The demographic and the societal context in which this research is taking place and changes being observed in the European region are described in Section 2, and the next three sections provide an overview of substantive and methodological issues related to ageing research in Europe: Section 3 describes the organisational aspects of ageing research in Europe; Section 4 provides a discussion of methodological developments in these research projects; and Section 5 outlines the major research and policy issues for the study of population ageing in current and future research. Section 6 describes the design and implementation of the PAU survey; Section 7 contains detailed abstracts for all of the research projects covered in this report, organised within topical areas; and Section 8 summarizes recommendations for future research as suggested by the investigators surveyed. The final section contains conclusions drawn from the present state of ageing research evaluated by the PAU survey and the suggestions made for the future. Finally, the appendices contain copies of the original survey documentation; an index that cross references the projects by country; and a list of contact addresses for each project.

1.3 Updates and Internet Dissemination

As noted above, this report represents the first attempt to catalogue ageing research projects in the ECE European member states. In an effort to revise and update information in a timely and accessible manner, the PAU intends to disseminate the information contained in this report on its World Wide Web site. This will allow the project inventory to be regularly updated to reflect new projects and additional information about existing research efforts. This format also will provide the means for information on new projects to be sent directly to the PAU and used to update the electronic versions of the directory. The contents of this report and information about the survey may be found at http://www.unece.org/pau/a_home. html.

To keep abreast of new developments and keep its databases up to date, the ECE relies upon researchers to provide them with information on new projects and to submit corrections and additional information on the projects listed in this report. For further information, please contact the Population Activities Unit at the following address:

> Survey on Ageing Research
> Population Activities Unit
> Economic Commission for Europe
> Palais des Nations
> CH-1211 Geneva 10
> Switzerland
> E-mail: Nikolai.Botev@UNECE.ORG

2 THE CHALLENGES OF POPULATION AGEING :
Recent Demographic Developments in Europe

All of the European countries covered in this report have completed demographic transitions in which the key vital rates of fertility and mortality have fallen from high to low levels. In the process, the levels of natural increase (crude birth rate minus crude death rate), experienced in the post-World War II period, also have declined. Figure 1 below shows that, for 14 of the 34 European countries for which the United Nations has published 1995 birth and death figures, negative rates of natural increase were reported (United Nations, 1996b). Most of the countries in which deaths exceeded births have been experiencing population declines as well, because net international migration has failed to compensate for the deficits in natural increase. In the main, low and negative natural increase is a function of historically-unprecedented low fertility levels, although in the Russian Federation and several other Eastern European countries, mortality also has risen and life expectancy declined.

Figure 1
Birth and Death Rates, European Countries, 1995

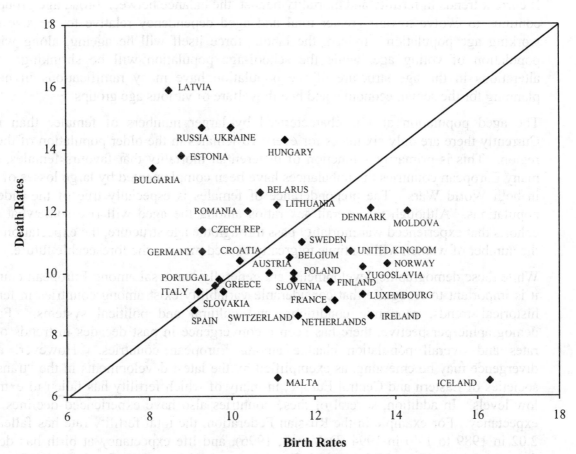

Source: World Population Prospects (The 1994 Revision). United Nations. New York, 1995.

Population ageing is a normal by-product of demographic transition, but the tempo of the process is a reflection both of past and current fertility, as well as improvements in survival, especially at advanced ages. All of the countries of Europe are ageing, as reflected in the growing numbers and proportion of older persons (65 years and over), and the increasing median age of the total population. These changes in population structure are moderate at present, but will accelerate rapidly as cohorts from the baby-boom generations become older in the second decade of the next century. Figure 2 on page 6 reveals that even countries with lower relative proportions of aged population will experience large proportional increases by the year 2030. Thus, population ageing will be the characteristic demographic feature of European societies for at least the next 35 years.

The aged population, itself, also has been ageing, with growing numbers of persons at the oldest-old ages, 85 and above. Currently the oldest-old represent slightly over 20 percent of the total aged population in the region. While the growing proportions of oldest-old will be attenuated by the arrival of large entry cohorts in the aged population, their numbers are likely to continue increasing as survival improves at advanced ages and the large cohorts succeed into the very oldest old age groups (Myers, 1994). The growth of the oldest-old has important policy implications, inasmuch as persons at these advanced ages tend to be potentially vulnerable to health and economic hardships.

If current trends in fertility and mortality persist, the balance between broad age groups will continue to evolve toward greater total and aged dependency relative to the size of the working age population. Indeed, the labour force itself will be ageing, along with the population of voting age, while the school-age population will be shrinking. These alterations in the age structure of the population have many ramifications in national planning for the social, economic and health welfare of various age groups.

The aged population also is characterised by larger numbers of females than males. Currently there are only six males for every 10 females in the older population of the ECE region. This is primarily a function of differential mortality that favours females, but in many European countries the imbalances have been complemented by large losses of males in both World Wars. The preponderance of females is especially true of the oldest-old populations. Although the overall sex ratios among the aged will rise somewhat as the cohorts that experienced war mortality pass through the age structure, the expectation is that the number of women will continue to greatly exceed men for the foreseeable future.

While these demographic developments are generally universal among European countries, it is important to recognise that considerable variability exist among countries in terms of historical trends, economic conditions, and cultural and political systems. From a demographic perspective, there has been a convergence in past decades in trends of vital rates and overall population change among European countries. However, a new divergence may be emerging, as exemplified by the latest developments in the "transition" societies of Eastern and Central Europe, in many of which fertility has fallen to extremely low levels. In addition, several of these countries also have experienced declines in life expectancy. For example in the Russian Federation, the total fertility rate has fallen from 2.02 in 1989 to 1.40 in 1994 (DaVanzo, 1996), and life expectancy at birth has declined from 64.9 in 1987 to 57.6 in 1994 for males and 74.3 to 71.2 for females (Council of Europe, 1996). The net impact of these declines in life expectancy is to retard, to some extent, the population ageing that would be expected from decreases in the total fertility rates. The increases in mortality, however, have been concentrated in the working ages, and thus are not likely to affect the median age of the population as much as fertility, but rather the proportions surviving to the older ages. The overall pattern therefore, is of continued negative population growth and toward increased ageing of the population.

Moreover, in several Southern European countries, such as Italy and Portugal, fertility has fallen to fairly stable levels considerably below replacement. Some of the Scandinavian countries, Sweden in particular, which experienced increased fertility in the early 1990s, now show a declining pattern. Thus, the overall demographic outlook is for increasing population ageing in all of the countries in the region; trends that will be exacerbated by large cohorts of persons succeeding into the older population in the next century.

Another demographic factor of considerable significance is the internal geographic distribution of older persons in national populations. Many countries in Europe still have relatively large proportions (30-50%) of their populations of all ages living in rural areas, in spite of strong urbanisation trends. In general, the proportions of the overall older population living in rural areas are even greater in these countries. Recent UN statistics reveal that the proportions of rural population who are 65 years and over exceed those of the urban population in all the European countries reported, except for Austria, the Netherlands, and Switzerland (Demographic Yearbook, 1996a.). The presence of large numbers of rural elderly can present particular problems in providing adequate health and other social service programs for older persons.

Figure 2
Percentage of Population 65 Years of Age and Over, European Countries, 1995 and 2030

Percentage

3   ORGANISATIONAL SUPPORT FOR EUROPEAN AGEING RESEARCH

It is instructive to characterise the structure of support that the research community in various European countries has provided for investigating these emerging ageing issues. Some examples of the organisational support for social science research on ageing are described below.

Although no European country has, as yet, created a separate governmental agency for co-ordinating research on a broad range of ageing issues, such as the National Institute on Aging in the United States, in a number of countries national programs on ageing have been instituted in the 1990s; notably in Italy, the Netherlands and Switzerland. The Italian National Research Council (CNR) created a comprehensive Targeted Project on Aging in 1991, in which competitively-awarded grants were made to institutions around the country in the biomedical and social science fields. One project is the *Italian Longitudinal Study of Aging (ILSA)*, a multicentre investigation involving eight research sites co-ordinated by the University of Florence. In the Netherlands, the Ministry of Education and Sciences and the Ministry of Welfare, Health and Cultural Affairs launched a *Netherlands Program of Research on Aging (NESTOR)* in 1989. One of the express goals of this programme was "to strengthen the position of gerontological research in the Netherlands with special emphasis on scientific infrastructure and international collaboration." The projects on *Living Arrangements and Social Networks of Older Persons (NESTOR-LSN)*, *Economic Aspects of Aging (CERRA)*, and *The Groningen Longitudinal Aging Study (GLAS)*, are all supported under this program. Finally, the Swiss National Science Foundation (SNSF) and the National Research Programme (NRP) created a six-year National Research Programme on Ageing in 1992. This program currently is supporting over two dozen research projects on the social, economic and health aspects of older persons.

Several cross-national research projects have been organised by United Nations agencies and other multinational organisations to investigate ageing issues. The European Office of the World Health Organisation (WHO) in 1979 sponsored studies on ageing in 15 European countries. These studies are still continuing in seven countries as follow-up investigations, known as the *European Longitudinal Study on Ageing (ELSA)*. In 1991, the European Union (EU) created an Observatory on Ageing and Older People within the framework of its Programme of Actions on Older People. The Observatory is intended to provide overview reports on specific issues in ageing drawing on a network of experts from the EU member states. Although the Observatory does not organise research as such, it serves to stimulate national and cross-national research that will answer important policy questions that the EU may address. The *SENECA Study On Nutrition Of Older Persons* is another cross-national investigation supported by the EU that involves a large number of European countries. Another EU initiative has been proposed recently (the *EuGeron* project) that would involve longitudinal studies in 14 EU countries and three Eastern European countries. The plan is to begin these studies in 1997-98.

The Economic Commission for Europe, with support from the United Nations Fund for Population Activities (UNFPA) and the U.S. National Institute on Aging (NIA), has since the 1980s devoted part of the program of the Population Activities Unit to co-ordinating studies of population ageing and its implications in member countries. More recently, it has directed the Dynamics of Population Ageing project that is designed to produce comparable microdata census samples for the round of 1990 censuses that were conducted in European countries, including both those in Western and Eastern Europe (including countries of the former USSR). This report also is an activity executed by the ECE, and supported by the United Nations Fund for Population Activities (UNFPA) and the U.S. National Institute on

Aging (NIA).

The research programs promoted by national governments and international organisations, do not in any way eclipse long-standing research contributions that are being made by individual scholars, institutes, and centres located in government agencies, Academies of Science, and universities, both within and across countries. Indeed, these efforts constitute the bulk of the social science research in the field of ageing. It is important to recognise that most universities in Europe are public institutions supported by national governments and it is through university administration that much of government support flows to research activities, however, a number of these university projects also are supported by funds from private foundations. For example, *The Bonn Aging Study (BOLSA),* an early longitudinal study, has been located in the Department of Psychology of the University of Bonn. Another longitudinal study in Germany, the Berlin Ageing Study (BASE), has been conducted by the Max Planck Institute for Human Development, with support from the Berlin-Brandenburg Academy of Sciences. Several studies in England have been sponsored by Age Concern England and Help the Aged, both of which are private foundations. In France, the French National Centre for Scientific Research has supported since 1972 the Life Course of Two Cohorts of Retirees of Greater Paris, an ongoing study.

There also exist a number of independent cross-national research programs in which one of the stipulated goals is to provide comparative analyses of the conditions of older persons in various European countries. The Luxembourg Income Study and the Luxembourg Employment Study are two such efforts that make use of cross-sectional surveys conducted over multiple time points in various countries. A number of comparative studies have been undertaken in the Scandinavian countries, especially with support from the Nordic Ministers and the Nordic Academy for Advanced Study. The *Nordic Research on Ageing (NORA)* project has been implemented in communities in Denmark, Finland, and Sweden. Other studies, such as the Daily Life Among the Old-Old and Oldest Old-A Nordic Comparative Study project, has been undertaken in Finland, Norway and Sweden. The four Nordic countries are included in the project on Adult Education for the Elderly in Scandinavia. The Network on Health Expectancy, known as REVES (Reséau Expérance de Vie en Santé), has involved a large number of investigators in various countries, including many in Europe, to develop comparable measures of healthy life expectancy for countries over time and for regional and other social and economic sub-groups. One aim of REVES has been to stimulate health surveys, including longitudinal investigations, to obtain standardised measures of disability and health status of older persons.

4 METHODOLOGICAL DEVELOPMENTS IN RECENT AGEING RESEARCH

The research projects detailed in this report, selective as they are, provide evidence of considerable activity across a broad range of substantive topics in the field of ageing. The research is on both the micro- (individual) level as well as macro- (aggregate) level, with each having a long historical record of development in the social sciences in European countries. A useful way of characterising these studies is to examine what sources of data and research designs are used. These include data from secondary, primary and linked sources; analysed through cross-sectional, cohort-comparison, longitudinal, and time-series designs as well as other innovative and experimental methods.

4.1 Research Design Issues

a) Secondary Data Analysis. The growth over the past decade of an extensive network of archives for storing and providing access to social science data in Europe has opened up promising opportunities for research on ageing, particularly comparative cross-national projects. Secondary analyses of survey data available through these archives or from independent researchers have come to play an increasingly important role in ageing research. For example, national surveys of economic conditions, such as income and employment, are being used to examine not only the life conditions of older persons, but also inter-generational variations. The *Luxembourg Income Study* and the *Luxembourg Employment Study* are prime examples of this approach. The *Russian Longitudinal Monitoring Study (RLMS)* proposes to use time-series data to examine the effects of changing social policies over time. Several of the studies we have reviewed provide access to their data through such regional archives. These include, among others, the Economic and Social Research Council (ESRC) Data Archive at the University of Essex in the United Kingdom, the Norwegian Social Science Data Services (SSDS) at the University of Bergen and the Swedish Social Science Data Service (SDS) at the University of Göteborg.

In addition, published census data and micro-data samples provide an opportunity to trace the dimensions of population ageing in terms of the changing age and sex structures of the total population, and the growth, composition, and geographic distribution of the aged population. An important recent development for demographic, social and economic analysis has been the availability of public use microdata sets from census samples of households and/or individuals, from which data on families and individuals can be drawn. The *ECE Census Microdata Project* is an example of the efforts to obtain census sample data from the 1990 round of censuses and major national surveys in a large number of European countries. A major advantage of using such sources is that they provide large samples of the older population, include persons living both in the community and in institutions, and make it possible to assess intra-household dimensions. In the United Kingdom, there has been an ongoing project of following a sample of persons enumerated over several censuses and supplementing the information for these individuals with linked data from vital statistics. Although the samples include persons at all adult ages, the overall sample is sufficiently large as to make it possible to examine older persons independently. There also have been some research projects directed at analysing data for cohorts as they reach the older ages and progress through advanced older ages. Such efforts may prove especially valuable in tracing the changing characteristics of the new aged in the coming decades.

Several projects utilise vital statistics records to trace changing patterns of mortality. These provide important inputs for forecasting future mortality and even morbidity changes, as inferred from the information on death certificates on the cause of death. These are important steps in preparing population projections of the older population, their numbers, composition and geographic distribution. The study of *Oldest Old Mortality - Demographic Models and Analysis*, co-ordinated from Odense in Denmark, combines vital statistics, demographic, and experimental data to examine levels of longevity across time and among both human and animal populations. These researchers also make their data available through the Danish Data Archives.

b) Primary Data Collection. The major source of data for ongoing research on the older population comes from primary data collection efforts, especially surveys. Surveys provide cross-sectional information about older individuals that can be used to estimate the current conditions of life of older persons and prevalence levels of various health states. Repeated cross-sectional surveys have been particularly useful in examining time-series trends in these dimensions. The two surveys of older persons conducted by the Hungarian Central Statistical Office are of this design. Another example is the 1994 Swiss study on *The Autonomy of the Ageing Population in Switzerland*, conducted in Geneva and the Central Valais region, which replicates a study carried out 15 years ago in the same areas. Co-ordination among research groups also has promoted the use of existing survey instruments in new studies in other countries to promote cross-national comparisons. This approach has been commonly taken in the Nordic countries, and other examples include the replication of part of the questionnaire from the *Living Arrangements and Social Networks of Older Persons (NESTOR-LSN)* project in the Netherlands for use with a sample of older adults in Tuscany, Italy, and the replication of the U.S. *Panel Study of Income Dynamics (PSID)* by the *German Socio-Economic Panel (GSOEP)*.

Many of the new research initiatives in this Report are designed as longitudinal or panel designs. There has been a long tradition for such research in such countries as Sweden, the Netherlands, France, Germany and the United Kingdom. Studies underway in other countries are following these designs, which are vital in analysing the dynamic changes in the lives of persons as they age. Not all these types of studies were initially designed as prospective studies. In fact, it has been possible to conduct follow-up studies that re-interview persons included in an earlier cross-sectional survey. A study planned by the Central Bureau of Statistics in Israel, for example, involves a follow-up of surviving persons who participated in the *Elderly National Survey* twelve years earlier in 1985. The *Swedish Panel Study of Living Conditions of the Oldest Old (SWEOLD)* conducted in 1992 followed up on surviving persons who originally participated in a 1968 national study. A variant on this approach was the use of the *Dutch Living Arrangements and Social Networks of Older Persons (NESTOR-LSN)* study as a sampling frame for the *Longitudinal Aging Study Amsterdam (LASA)* study. The follow-up design is a relatively effective means of obtaining longitudinal data provided that locating earlier participants is accomplished effectively. *The availability of independent sources of information on the cause of deaths is beneficial for such studies.*

For longitudinal studies, an important design issue relates to the timing of re-interviewing waves. A two or three-year interval seems to be the most common among the projects reviewed in this report, but some studies have sought for more frequent contact. An interesting innovation has been included in the *Groningen Longitudinal Aging Study (GLAS)*, where important events occurring to participants as reported by their general physicians trigger at least three repeated contacts with the person over a single year. Many of the more intensive community studies, such as the *Lund 80+ and Reykjavik* studies in Sweden and Iceland and the *Berlin Aging Study (BASE)*, involve even more frequent and intensive data collection encounters with participants. Several incorporate physician's clinical assessments at regular intervals in conjunction with self-reported survey responses, such as the *Italian Longitudinal Study of Aging (ILAS)*.

In addition to surveys that focus on individuals, there also some surveys of organisations. *The Economic Aspects of Aging (CERRA)* study in The Netherlands, which focuses on the retirement process, was accompanied by a survey of firms in which the individual survey respondents were employed. Other research is designed at the outset to involve both organisations and individuals. An example of this is The *Vulnerable Elderly and Elder Politics* study in Denmark that surveyed housing authorities as well as persons living in various types of living accommodations.

c) Mode of Interviewing. There are examples of all of the major approaches for data collection in the projects included in the Report. These include interviewing face-to-face, by telephone or mail; and by drop-off and pick-up, as well as the use of performance tests and bio-assays by clinical personnel. In addition, data collection may take place in a home, office, or clinical setting. In some studies, such as the *NORA* studies, data collection takes place in multiple settings, which makes it possible to assess response biases using different venues and types of measurement.

Computer Assisted Personal Interviewing (CAPI) and Computer Assisted Telephone Interviewing (CATI) is only used in a few countries, for example The Netherlands. However, it is likely that such equipment is likely to become much more widespread in years to come. A rather unique research design is that being followed in the *Dutch VSB Savings Project*, in which sample respondents use their personal computers at home to complete questionnaires that are fully computerised.

d) Use of Linked Data. Finally, it is important to note that some of the on-going studies involve linking individual survey information with data from such sources as death certificates, administrative records, pension funds, and general practitioners. This is a promising development in expanding the multidimensional aspects of the ageing process, but it is often the case that such efforts run into confidentiality restraints. Several studies in Israel have been able to match records. The *Life Course of Two Cohorts of Retirees of Greater Paris* also incorporates data from pension fund sources, vital statistics and surveys. The twin registry data from the *Swedish Adoption/Twin Study of Ageing (SATSA)* is matched regularly to sources of vital statistics in Sweden. Another ambitious effort to link data is the *Italian Longitudinal Study of Aging*, which obtains medical records from hospital discharges for study participants, as well as death information for decedents.

e) Disciplinary Focus. A distinctive feature of many newly-instituted studies, especially social, epidemiological, and biomedical investigations, is a broad multidimensional perspective that has been adopted to study transitions in the lives of older persons. This often entails a wide range of disciplinary perspectives and multiple types of assessments. The *ILSA* study in Italy involves household interviews, physical examinations, and laboratory tests. In addition, the project includes an inter-wave hospital discharge survey and a mortality follow-up. Several of the studies, such as the Melton Mowbray study, which focus on cognition and psychiatric disorders have involved both clinical assessments as well as personal interviewing. Moreover, physical performance tests have been introduced in a number of studies, so as to complement self-reports of functional limitations from interviews.

f) Sample Construction. Random sampling procedures are the norm for most of the surveys that are included in this report. In some community surveys, especially where a single-age cohort is sought, all persons fulfilling the criteria may be included. Adequate coverage in some studies may require oversampling from certain groups. This is particularly important in studies that are intended to cover all persons over a specified age or in an extended age range. Thus, in some studies, like the Italian *ILSA* project, equal numbers of persons in five-year age groups from ages 65-84. Such a procedure provides not only adequate cases at the advanced ages, but also ensures that there will be sufficient survivors for subsequent waves of a panel study.

The sampling frames used for the research projects in this survey vary widely. They include census listings, and the records of population and municipal registers, administrative records, and general practitioners files. Less common are aerial-based sampling that involves screening procedures. This may reflect the fact that centralised listings may be more widely available in many European countries than they are in North America, for example. It is generally accepted that list files provide more appropriate sampling frames for surveys than cluster sampling procedures which are frequently employed elsewhere.

g) Expanding the Unit of Analysis. An interesting development in several investigations has been the inclusion of other members of the household, in addition to the sample case, in study populations. This may be a spouse of the sample case or persons who provide care for a needy person. Interviewing multiple respondents in a household makes it possible to not only assess the reliability of responses, but also investigate family decision-making. A focus on intra-family dynamics is especially meaningful in examining such areas as retirement (where both spouses may be working), savings and expenditure patterns, health-care seeking, and informal family care giving. The emphasis on the family as a social unit would seem to be a important complement to much ageing research has mainly tended to focus on older individuals. Many surveys of older persons use proxies to obtain information about individuals who are unable to participate fully in the interviews. This design specifically incorporates such persons in the research, allowing studies that address the potential bias of proxy responses by proxy characteristics and relationship to the older respondent.

4.2 Generalizability of Results

One of the prevailing issues in ageing research has been how to balance the need for specificity on the cultural, physical, economic, and even genetic circumstances of ageing, and the importance of establishing patterns within representative populations. The applicability of results beyond their clinical relevance to national and cross-national populations is of great importance in ageing research at this time.

a) Geographic scope. Although many survey projects still focus on specific communities, there are clear indications that the national projects underway involving data collection conducted in multiple sites; thereby making the results more representative for the country as a whole. In addition, of course, there are other surveys that are national in scope, although relatively few such studies focus on older populations. The suitability of data on older persons from such samples depends on the initial size of the samples and their coverage of the persons at the advanced ages. The collection of national data on a more representative basis with co-ordinated data-collection strategies enable researchers to carry out comparative cross-national studies. It appears that some of the research undertakings of this type, such as the ECE census sample project and the recently initiated *EuGeron* project, include countries from both Eastern and Western Europe, thus enhancing comparative research on the conditions of life of older persons in quite different contexts.

b) Coverage of Age Groups and Birth Cohorts. The age groups selected for study range widely across various European studies. There has been a tradition in Scandinavia to select single-year cohorts for study. Thus, the early Gothenburg studies followed a panel that was aged 70 at entry. The *NORA* studies in Scandinavia focused on persons at age 75. The French Two Cohort Study selected persons who were born in 1907-12 and 1919-24, thus cohorts separated by roughly 13 years in age. It is interesting to note that many of the Swedish and other Scandinavian studies focus on persons at the oldest-old ages. In addition, there are numerous studies, a few of which are included in the report, that have concentrated on centenarians, a group of long importance to gerontologists. For studies that deal primarily with retirement, ages before and after retirement are the prime consideration. Thus, in the Dutch *CERRA* study the ages 53-63 are the selection criteria.

An important aspect of the study of older persons is to compare their conditions relative to those of younger persons. Surveys that include persons at all of the adult ages make these types of comparisons, such as the household surveys that are included in the Luxembourg Income Studies. The adequacy of such investigations rests on sufficiently large samples of older persons so as to make appropriate age and sex-based estimates.

Research employing a life course perspective focuses on specific stages in the individual's life course and the intersection of generations. Three-generation family studies have been one design that involves interviewing of members of a pivot generation at advanced middle ages, their parents and children. The French study of Relations between Generations and Family Support to Elderly People is an example of this approach. The main purposes of such an investigation are to obtain information about intergenerational exchanges, the types of support given to children as they complete schooling and enter the labour force, and the nature of parental support, especially financial and informal caregiving.

4.3 Model Specificity

For most of the research projects on a national scale, the aim is to be representative of all persons in the specified age groups. However, other research may have the specific intention of targeting selected groups of older persons. Some studies concentrate on women, who represent such a large proportion of the older population and who are particularly likely to be widowed and in need of social supports at the advanced ages. The *Belgian Women As They Age* project clearly had this intent. Other projects focus on the rural elderly, such as the *Bangor Longitudinal Study of Ageing* in Wales, or specifically include people living in rural settings, such as those living in Kibbutz in the *Israeli Cross-Sectional and Longitudinal Aging Study (CALAS)*. There are a number of studies that focus on older immigrant, ethnic, and racial groups. For example, The *German Socio-Economic Panel* has included an oversample of guest workers and new immigrants to the former West Germany. The *British Household Panel Study (BHPS)* also has been used for studies of immigrant populations. In fact, a notable feature of several studies in this report is the selection of sub-samples for special intensive investigations.

Most of the studies reviewed in this Report are limited to community-dwelling older persons. Very few include both community and institutional samples. This is particularly unfortunate when a goal of the research is to obtain nationally representative prevalence figures for health conditions, functional limitations, etc. Nonetheless, some of the longitudinal studies may begin as community-based samples, but include participants who enter institutions in subsequent periods

4.4 Replication and Standardization

There has been considerable progress made in developing standardized instruments for examining important conceptual areas in studies undertaken in different countries. In part this has arisen because of the sharing of research designs with investigations in other countries. For example, the *Panel Study of Income Dynamics (PSID)*, which has been conducted in the United States since 1975, has been used as a model for the *Dutch Socio-Economic Panel Study (DSEP)* and the *German Socio-Economic Panel (GSOEP)*, which began as a sample of persons in West Germany and now includes, as well, a sample of East Germans. Another study recently begun in The Netherlands, the *Economic Aspects of Aging (CERRA)* is modelled after *the Health and Retirement Study (HRS)* in the United States.

While the standardisation of instruments is generally more common in biomedical, epidemiological, psychiatric and nutritional surveys, there are encouraging signs that serious efforts are being made to create more comparable instruments in the social and economic fields as well. The projects carried out by the ECE and The *Luxembourg Income Study* to produce databases for comparative purposes illustrate the ways in which standardisation and harmonisation of basic measures can be accomplished using already existing data. In the former, census data, and in the latter, household survey data. A singular feature of each effort is the availability of data for households, as well as information about individuals.

4.5 Data Dissemination and Analysis

There has been growing interest in the ageing field for comparative research, both across countries and communities and across time. These developments have been spurred on by the increasingly broader dissemination of data for secondary analyses. Data archives have been organised to process data from studies and make them available either fully by electronic transmission or in computerised form, or on a more restrictive basis. A number of such archives exist in Europe and there have been recent efforts to co-ordinate their efforts with such groups as the National Archive for Computerized Data on Aging (NACDA) located at the University of Michigan in the United States. The nine exploratory Centers for the Demography of Aging sponsored by the U.S. National Institute on Aging also have an important role in making data available to researchers around the world.

The survey used for this report obtained information about the availability of data from the various studies. Over half of the participating organisations indicated a willingness to share data, although several impose specific restrictions upon access or use. Two of the projects, the *Luxembourg Income Study* and the *ECE sample census* effort, have the express aim of providing data for cross-national analyses to investigators who participate in their research programs. While certain research groups resist sharing data and, in some cases, lay down legal obstacles, there is likely to be considerable movement towards greater collaboration and cross-study analyses in the years ahead. Studies that share data with the research community are likely to have increased publication rates and receive greater attention. These trends towards greater collaboration and exchange of research findings is, in large part, due to the growing number of researchers in the ageing field and the professional exchanges stimulated by such groups as the International Association of Gerontology, which convenes periodic regional meetings and international congresses. Anyone wishing to obtain access to a dataset described in this report should contact project investigators directly (see Appendix 11.6 for addresses).

The dissemination of user-friendly software for statistical analysis has contributed to the rapid acceptance and use of multivariate statistical techniques. Structural equation modelling of the important dimensions affecting the lives of older persons provide increasingly sophisticated methods to establish relationships between these dimensions and the ageing processes involved. The use of survival analyses and other dynamic modelling approaches have come into wider use to deal with temporal data that has become common with panel types of studies. In general, there has been a convergence in statistical approaches across disciplines in the past two decades and these developments will no doubt continue in the years ahead.

There also has been considerable development of household modelling, especially in France, The Netherlands, and Poland. This research, often involving event-history analyses and multistate life table approaches, provides important inputs into projections of changing family forms. While modelling of these processes at the older ages have not been fully implemented, the availability of longitudinal data for larger samples should permit many such efforts in the future.

More limited has been the development of linkages between survey data and administrative records in European countries. The usefulness of current databases as well as future data collection efforts would be enhanced by efforts to join death records, health care utilisation data, earnings files and insurance information to household surveys.

5   MAJOR THEMES IN SOCIAL SCIENCE RESEARCH ON AGEING IN EUROPE

Accelerating population ageing has placed pressure on the ability to maintain social protection for increasingly large older cohorts. This policy issue in particular has generated heightened awareness of and interest in ageing phenomena. The importance of accurate and detailed information about the aged population and the ageing process for forecasting future developments has called attention to gaps in our present knowledge.

From modest beginnings in the immediate post-World War II period, social science research in the field of ageing has developed rapidly in the past few decades. Recent developments have been characterised by deepening interest in the traditional disciplines of economics, political science, psychology and sociology, as well as multidisciplinary research efforts that involve cognate fields, such as demography, epidemiology, public health and the policy sciences. It is a fair judgement, even in recent years, that much of the social and bio-medical research in ageing has been problem-driven rather than theory-driven.

Nonetheless, the research being conducted in Europe in the 1990s shows considerable evidence of the conceptual and methodological developments emerging in social science approaches to ageing research. Projects surveyed in this report tend to take a comprehensive approach to ageing: some incorporate a life course approach; others are designed to conduct explicit tests of the relationships of social and economic factors to health and mortality; others still test economic theories about life-cycle patterns of work, leisure, and savings. A number of recent studies have undertaken the daunting research task of using multidiscipinary approaches and longitudinal designs.

A review of these diverse projects reveals a number of themes of research and policy importance. These themes are outlined in the sections below.

5.1 Health and Mortality

a) Functional Health and disability. The measurement and comparison of trajectories of health and functioning, prevalence of disease and disability, and population level measures of healthy life expectancy are all important aspects of health that need to be understood, and its importance is clearly reflected in the focus of the studies examined in this report. How the mortality changes of the past century are linked to changes in the onset and progression of disease and its consequences for functional health is a central question both in our understanding of ageing and in projecting future health care needs and costs.

The largest number of projects in this survey focused on health-related issues (25). Several of these approach health and disability broadly, such as the *European Longitudinal Study of Aging (ELSA)*, *Aging in Leganés*, the *Longitudinal Aging Study Amsterdam (LASA)*, or the *Melton Mowbray Ageing Project*. Others focus on specific aspects of health, such as the *DiComano study of cardiac failure*, and Kuznetsova's study of *Ethnicity and Ageing in the Ukraine*, which focuses on risk factors for cardiovascular diseases.

The *SATSA* project and the twins studies in the *Odense Oldest-Old Mortality project* take a different approach, using samples of twins to draw inferences about the genetic and environmental influences on health at older ages. In addition, several of the multidisciplinary projects, such as the *Berlin Ageing Study (BASE)*, employ broad approaches to examine the social, psychological and economic correlates of health and disability.

b) Healthy life expectancy. The concept of Healthy Life Expectancy has been developed as an indicator of the health of a population, which reflects not only the role of mortality in defining population health, but also the increase in chronic morbidity and disability that accompanies population ageing. HLE incorporates disability rates into life table estimates of age-specific survival. It represents the number of years an individual may expect to live in good health, out of the total number of years remaining. Cross-national comparisons of healthy life expectancy, such as those being developed by the REVES (Reséau Expérance de Vie en Santé) and time series estimates of ALE and HLE like those being derived by Brønnum-Hansen in *Developments In Health Expectancy In Denmark*, will be extremely useful in developing an understanding of the dynamics of morbidity and mortality change across time and countries.

c) **Differential Mortality and Longevity**. In recent years, there has been renewed interest in assessing socio-economic differentials in mortality, as more detailed data linking measures of social class, health behaviours and mortality by cause are becoming available. In addition, cross-national comparative studies have become increasingly important in our understanding of the potential reductions in adult mortality that may be accomplished. For example, using data from the *Odense Oldest-Old Mortality project,* Manton and Vaupel (1995) compared survival above age 80 in five developed countries, and speculate with regard to behavioural differences that might lead to an advantage observed in the United States in oldest-old survival.

Understanding the determinants of variation in human longevity is of great importance, and new biological and genetic data will provide tremendous opportunities for social science researchers to link socio-economic and environmental observations to biological measures. Increasing cross-national variability in mortality and changes over time, also creates great opportunities for research, as appropriate data is collected (Christensen and Vaupel, 1996).

d) **Health Behaviours**. Acceptance of scientific research about diet, smoking, and exercise has changed norms and attitudes about health behaviours in most of the developed world. Prolonged research on the effects of smoking has taken place in Europe, but factors such as diet and physical activity are now receiving increasing amounts of attention. For example, the *CALAS* project focuses on risk factors, including behavioural and lifestyle influences, for health transitions. Additional longitudinal and time-series studies also are needed to examine the extent to which cohorts have altered their preventive activities and the consequences of such changes for health outcomes at older ages. It seems likely that much of the data being collected now in studies of health described in this report, will provide the information needed for such analyses.

e) **Projections of health, disability, and mortality**. A major question to be addressed is forecasting future health status and mortality for the current working age cohorts. This is an important but complex proposition. It involves a long list of assumptions (and research questions) about the ways in which adult morbidity incidence and prevalence will change, how these changes are linked to survival probabilities, and how these morbidity-mortality linkages are mediated by early life health and health behaviours. In addition, there are important issues about the influence of health care technology, environmental change, differential access to health care, and a host of unobserved differences among subgroups. A project which is seeking to answer these questions for Europe is Wolfgang Lutz' *Alternative Population Projections For Major World Regions*. However, the future dynamics of morbidity and disability need to be more fully explored.

5.2 Economic Issues

a) Social security, pensions, and the future of the welfare state. The implications of slowing economic growth and transformations in political systems since 1975 have heightened the interest by policy-makers in the role of social security and other government benefits for the well-being of older persons. In most European nations, the state provides extensive benefits to the aged in the form of public pensions, health care, and housing. However, the underlying demographic pressures of population ageing have led to concerns about over-reliance on welfare systems.

In the Western European countries, private pensions are already in place, although the balance and mix of public and private resources and their differential distribution in the aged population has not been fully investigated. The share of financing for pensions supported by the state has historically been highest in eastern European countries, while in western Europe, employees have proportionally contributed more towards their pensions (Kinsella and Gist, 1995). In the eastern Europe, private enterprise is only beginning to be developed, and the ways in which the economic reforms will be implemented and how private sources for pension income will be developed are major questions in this area.

Some arguments have been made to propose that the strength of the welfare state has itself been the cause of other social and demographic changes by eroding norms of personal responsibility, but most economic and demographic literature does not provide much support for this contention, and the general conclusion of researchers appears to be that the welfare state is an important and valuable means of social support and should be preserved (Ploug, 1994). In recent years, many European countries have scaled back social benefits and reduced the eligibility of some types of health care for full public payment. In some countries, the patient's responsibility for health care costs also has been increased. However, in most cases, the older population as a group has continued to receive substantial benefits. Such changes in the policy environment will provide opportunities to investigate the role of the state in more depth.

Extensive study of the implications of past trends and future impact of policy changes are sorely needed. Several studies in this report examine the economic well-being of the elderly. The majority of these studies take a micro-approach focusing on the financial security of individuals. These include the *Luxembourg Income Study* (whose data also have been used for macro-level cross-national comparisons), and *the Dutch* and *German Socio-Economic panels (DSEP and GSOEP)*, both of which are similar to the U.S. Panel Study of Income Dynamics, and focus on the dynamic changes in income and wealth across the life cycle. Prinz' study of *Inter-Generational Equity in Pension Systems*, on the other hand, applies a macro-economic and demographic approach to develop models of pension and population change from the past (since 1920) to the distant future (to 2080).

Additional macroeconomic models of inputs to economic growth should be developed to assess some of the implications of political and economic changes for the older population. Additional cross-national information on individual and household economics also should be collected, to complement the strengths that already exist in this research area.

b) Savings Rates. Population ageing is generally expected to depress the national household savings rate. This relationship, however, is contingent upon the cohort specific saving and dissaving behaviours actually observed. For example, newly retired persons may not dissave if they anticipate health care costs or expect to leave bequests. In addition, the rates at which working age individuals (and households) are saving, given current economic conditions, is an important indicator of expected post-retirement wealth and a necessary component of policy which seeks to reduce dependence upon government provided social security. However, savings rates are themselves responsive not only to anticipated lifetime income and consumption, but also to the structure of available benefits from the state. The potential interplay of demographic-economic changes with policy shifts is an important area to examine.

The Economics Institute at Tilburg University in the Netherlands is examining savings behaviour through the *VSB Savings Project*, which adds information about assets and consumption behaviour to the *Dutch Socio-Economic Panel* described above. They are also engaged in several other analyses of savings behaviour, based on analysis of survey data and laboratory experiments on financial decision-making.

c) Retirement and the ageing of the labour force. In Western Europe, policymakers have paid attention to the use of incentives for early retirement to reduce the existing high levels of youth unemployment, and to decrease the overall size of the labour force in times of restructuring. In Eastern Europe, low fertility has led to concerns about a shrinking labour force, and interest in providing disincentives to withdrawal from the labour force among older workers. These changes also need to be assessed in terms of the predominant industries and occupations in each country and how they have evolved over time. Where rapid change or industrial restructuring has taken place, the age structure of the labour force will be particularly important in mediating the impacts on the well-being of the population. Age is a significant factor in productivity in some trades and not in others and can, in fact, in some occupations may increase productivity. Research on the role of incentives for retirement behaviour includes the CERRA study of *Economic Aspects of Ageing*, which examines retirement transitions as a response to financial incentives. Huuhtanen's study of *Work And Retirement Among Older Workers In Finland* takes a somewhat different approach by examining retirement expectations among both the working age population and recent retirees.

Retirement is of interest to researchers not only in terms of its timing and the subsequent implications for unemployment rates or the receipt of pension and health benefits, but also as a life course transition. In this sense, the nature of the retirement process (incorporating bridge jobs, part-time work and re-employment in different industries) is important to understand, as are more general questions about the quality of retirement and how increased survival has transformed the post-employment period of individual lives (Wise, 1996). Schneider's study of *Retirement Transitions in Switzerland* is one example of this approach. In this project, information on social networks and personality characteristics were collected in order to examine the process of adaptation to retirement. A major survey also is being undertaken by the *OPCS* in England to study a representative sample of persons as they make the transition to and through retirement. Cribier's study of the *Life Course Of 2 Cohorts Of Retirees Of The Greater Paris Region* also seeks to combine economic and social information in order to examine quality of retirement.

d) Labour Force and Retirement Migration. One way in which migration has always been acknowledged to be of importance to the well-being of the older population is in the implications of changing migration patterns among the working age population. Migration towards economic opportunity among younger workers affects the situation of older persons 'left behind', often in rural areas. In most of the countries in Europe migration flows have separated families and altered the patterns of informal support available. Many countries in Europe, especially those of Eastern European region, have large proportions of the older population living in rural areas.

Migration flows also take place internationally. The flows of workers, both skilled and unskilled, across national borders has led to shifts in the presence of foreign workers, displaced persons, and legal migrants across countries and increased the diversity of ethnicity in many European nations, yet relatively little research has examined the process of population ageing in the context of such increasing ethnic and racial diversity.

Of additional importance in the European region, however, is the geographic movement of older persons. As healthier and more active cohorts withdraw from the labour force, increasing mobility among the older population may be observed. Such streams include migration among the newly retired towards family or to leisure communities. They also may represent movements towards forms of assistance, such as migration across geo-political boundaries to countries with more comprehensive old age benefits, residential change to be near family members for support and contact, or into age-graded housing, supportive, or long-term care communities. Warnes and colleagues are studying such population movements in their project on *International Retirement Migration of Britons to Southern Europe*. This project provides a good example of research that can be done to study the decision-making process involved in retirement migration as well as the effects of migrating on the individual, the sending, and the receiving areas.

5.3 Social Aspects

a) Implications of the evolving status and roles of women. There has been recognition of the important role that women's increasing labour force participation has had on the modes of family organisation over the course of this century. Of direct importance is the effect on the availability of informal care for older persons with long-term care needs. One area that has not been so fully investigated is the potential effect on economic growth if policies are implemented that "encourage" women to provide informal care to older family members and work at part-time or informal sector activities, rather than as skilled labour.

Another aspect of this change that is usually less closely observed by researchers is the effect of women's increasing participation in the labour force for their own economic and care needs in the future. As more economically active women age, they may be expected to bring to retirement independent resources formerly not available to them, such as private pensions and savings. Ostner (1993) has argued that many of the social policy reforms that have taken place over the last decade have only minimally affected women's economic well-being because they have focused on market-based reforms to remove obstacles to free trade between European nations. European Courts, therefore, may have been the most effective agent in improving women's status in the European Union, by rendering decisions that have improved women's employment status, and therefore their access to market reforms.

Because women have traditionally been *both* the main providers and main recipients of care, any trends that improve women's economic well-being through increased personal savings and access to private pension income can substantially transform the long-term care picture for the better. The reports prepared by Dooghe and colleagues on *Women as they Age*; and *Elderly Women in Europe* provide a preliminary comparison of the status of older women in Europe, but new data should be collected in order to evaluate the changing position of older women over time, and through policy changes and economic restructuring.

b) Transformations of family patterns. In several European countries, the family has been formally recognised in legislation and policy as a fundamental social institution. The national constitutions of Finland, France, Germany, Greece, Ireland, Italy, Luxembourg, Portugal, and Spain all explicitly mention the obligation of support by the state to the family, often defining the "family" by the presence of a married couple and focusing on family within households (Hantrais and Letablier, 1996).

Yet the diversity of family structures observed in European countries has increased rapidly over the past decade. Rising levels of cohabitation, increasing levels of divorce and remarriage, and the increasing presence of women as heads of households, have transformed not only the living arrangements of older persons, but the entire network of social relations in which they are embedded. In addition, increased joint survival of spouses and siblings within families has altered the patterns of family structure and support. Parents and children have new opportunities to develop adult relationships together and healthy, prosperous grandparents are becoming increasingly important as providers of instrumental, emotional, and financial assistance to their children and grandchildren.

The effects of such demographic changes on the balance of family and state responsibility for long-term care and economic security of the elderly continues to be of great importance. One of the main policy concerns driving interest in the consequences of population ageing-- perhaps the overarching question--is the way in which declining fertility and increased survival at older ages combine to reduce the capacity of the family to provide economic support and physical care to older persons and shift the burden increasingly to the state. These demographic transformations have occurred at the same time as economic growth has stabilised in most countries and structures of social protection have undergone extensive scrutiny through the evolution of the European Union (EU).

Some of the projects concerned with family change and social policy include: *Relations Between Generations And Family Support To Elderly People,* which focuses on relations within multigenerational families; *Living Arrangements And Social Networks Of Older Adults (NESTOR-LSN),* and *The Bangor Longitudinal Study Of Ageing,* both of which focus on change in social networks over time and their effects on health and well-being; and *The Russia Longitudinal Monitoring Survey (RLMS)* which is specifically concerned with the effects of changing policy on the quality of life of older persons. Several studies of health and well-being, such as *The Longitudinal Aging Study Amsterdam; Reykjavik 80+: A Longitudinal Study Of 80 Year-Olds And Older In Iceland;* and *the Elderly Aged 60 And Over In Households In Israel* also report that they collected data on family structure in their studies..

c) Social Networks, Household Structure, and Living Arrangements. Population ageing has played a large part in the rise in number of households and the decrease in their size in recent years, as well as the increasing prevalence of non-family households. Better health and availability of housing accommodations also have played a part in increasing the ability of older persons to live independently in the community for longer. The proportions living alone within the older population also have consequently increased. Such trends have led to a focus in research on the relationships between living arrangements and social support, especially with a focus on the role of social networks. This approach is exemplified in the *NESTOR-LSN* project, and the *Bangor Longitudinal Study,* as well as being a component of many other projects.

d) Housing. Small-scale studies of environmental design and housing modifications are frequently undertaken with regard to the special needs of the elderly and Europe, particularly Scandinavia, leads the world in the conceptualisation of assisted-living. However, the importance of housing as an area of demographic research has not been deeply examined. Few large scale studies were identified that considered the role of housing as a component in the long-term care system, or as a reflection of changing social norms about family life, or of economic needs. Yet, the implications of changing housing supply and demand, as well as its quality and accessibility, are important components in projections of health care needs and economic growth. Retirement migration has created new markets for small environmentally manageable housing units, and the desire by most older persons for "intimacy at a distance", or the ability to live close to, but not in the same household as their relatives, should spur the development of new studies that take these changes into account. None of the studies examined in this survey focused on issues directly related to housing in the community.

e) Social-Psychology and Human Development. Some of the most prominent work in the areas of social-psychology of ageing and the of the life-course approach to the study of human development and individual ageing has taken place in Europe. The life course approach to ageing focuses on how the timing and sequencing of events experienced over an individual or cohort's lifetime affects their ageing process and also the diversity of the older population. These perspectives have often led researchers to focus on longitudinal studies of small purposive samples (such as Seims' study of *Teenagers reaching retirement age*), but a few of the studies included in this report are examining large representative samples, such as the study of *Daily Life among the Oldest-Old* by Andersson, and the Kohlis' *German Ageing Survey*.

f) Education The role of education with regard to the ageing process and the well-being of the elderly has taken on several meanings. The first is strongly related to the life course approach to ageing, and examines the ways in which education is a lifelong process by which older persons can continue to participate in both formal and informal educational activities after retirement, in ways that improve the quality of their lives, maintain intellectual activity and increase personal growth. A second focus of importance in research on education is in terms of its importance in retraining the ageing labour force to adapt to changing economic conditions and job opportunities. None of the studies identified through this survey have examined this question.

5.4   Health Care Service Use

a) Health Care Expenditures. The social and economic changes that accompany the process of population ageing have important implications for the demands that will be made on formal health care systems, as well as the increasing need for long-term care services. The provision of acute health care services has been a strong commitment in most member nations. Even where efforts have been made to contain social expenditures, health care has been largely untouched. However, the organisation of health care systems and costs of services vary both across and within countries.

b) Long-Term Care and Institutionalisation. Addressing the provision of medical and personal home care for the older population is a primary concern for Europe. Substantial variation in the mechanisms for funding such care may be found across the continent. A large number of countries make use of financial incentives to promote the use of community-based long term care. Finland, France, Sweden, and the United Kingdom provide payments to disabled elderly in the community and also compensate informal care givers; Austria, Germany, and the Netherlands make payments to the recipient only, and support is given to the provider only in Belgium, Denmark, Ireland, and Italy (Jones, and Millar, 1996). Long-term care insurance policies to fund home care are being investigated in the France, Germany, and the Netherlands, as are family leave policies for both elder and child care in several countries. In some countries, policies are being developed to limit new construction of nursing homes, thereby limiting the number of institutional beds and pressing for alternative options. Monitoring the implications of such policies for quality of care will be essential in the future.

Several studies in this survey focus on factors enhancing the capacity for community care. Several of these are evaluating policy changes. For example, Radebold's study of *Rural Elderly Needing Care* is interested in the extension of home care services to rural Germany, Noro's examination of *The Use Of Open And Institutional Care Policies For The Dependent Elderly* studies the effectiveness of de-institutionalization policies in Finland, and Jegede's study of *Transportation for the Elderly* investigates the role of transportation policies in England. Social factors are of importance as well. For example, Justel's project *Informal Support For The Elderly* is examining the role of the extended family in providing informal care in Spain.

Although institutionalisation and policies about institutional care were the major focus for only two projects: *The Use Of Open And Institutional Care Policies For The Dependent Elderly;* and *Acceptance And Benefits Of Extended In-Home Services For Rural Elderly Needing Care,* several studies examined differential institutionalization rates among their respondents as a project outcome (*The Cross-Sectional And Longitudinal Ageing Study: (CALAS), Aging In Leganés , The Berlin Ageing Study (BASE) ,* and *The Autonomy Of The Ageing Population In Switzerland*). In addition, the *Melton Mowbray Ageing Project* and the *Bangor Longitudinal Study Of Ageing* conducted follow-up interviews with respondents who were institutionalised over the study period.

6   DESIGN AND IMPLEMENTATION OF THE SURVEY ON AGEING RESEARCH IN EUROPE

The Survey on Ageing Research in Europe comprised two waves of data collection. The goal of Wave I was to take stock of the wide range of ageing-related research in Europe. The first questionnaires were administered in October, 1995 to a list of researchers in major universities, research institutes, and demographic centres throughout the region compiled by the PAU of the ECE. Subsequently, a snowball technique was used, in which respondents in the initial mailing were asked to identify additional projects to be included in the survey. These questionnaires were distributed between December, 1995 and March, 1996.

Each institution surveyed received a short questionnaire on diskette designed to record information on the subject area, funding resources, and type of research being conducted (see Appendix 11.1.1). Respondents were instructed to identify projects on demographic, social, gerontological, economic, health, and epidemiological aspects of ageing. Projects of all sizes were considered eligible for inclusion, with the exception of medical studies such as clinical trials or tests of new therapeutic interventions. The final collection of Wave I questionnaires represents 316 projects from about 150 institutions and individuals.   The responses to this phase of the survey have been published by the ECE in the *Directory of Ageing Research in the ECE* .

The goal of the second wave of the survey was to compile more detailed information on large scale research efforts, those using innovative research strategies, or involving primary data collection with high-quality survey instruments. A more detailed questionnaire was mailed to the principal investigators of approximately 50 of these projects between February and May 1996, requesting information about the goals and activities of their respective research projects, and specific queries on survey methods and data quality (See Appendix 11.1.2). Additional information collected included institutional history, information about collaborative ventures, and their views on the future directions for ageing research in Europe. A total of 44 responses were received, analysed and entered into a database maintained at the PAU. The information was thereafter used in the present report. All of the responses that were returned to the ECE were included in preparation of the present report, and the contents in entirety have been compiled in a database held by the PAU. The entries in this report and in the databases are presented with minimal editing as supplied by the investigators themselves and represent the status of the projects as of the date of the survey. More recent information may be obtained by contacting the principal investigators directly (see Appendix 11.6), or from the ECE web site, as project leaders update their entries.

One of the goals of the surveys was to identify and characterise the research efforts in as many European countries as possible. To this end, additional projects were identified through consultation with experts, and added to those already surveyed for inclusion in this report. The information provided by the principal investigators also was supplemented from published sources as available and appropriate.

7. PROJECTS BY SUBJECT AREA

7.1 HEALTH AND MORTALITY

7.1.1 LONGITUDINAL AGING STUDY AMSTERDAM (LASA)
Dorly J. H. Deeg, Principal Investigator
Vrije Universiteit, Amsterdam, The Netherlands
Dates: 1991 - 2000

The Longitudinal Aging Study Amsterdam (LASA) is designed to be an interdisciplinary longitudinal study. The main topics of concern are autonomy and quality of life of older persons. Autonomy is defined as observed physical, cognitive, emotional and social functioning. Quality of life is defined as the evaluation by older persons of their functioning in each of these domains. The four components of functional capacity will have different and interrelated contributions to autonomy and quality of life. The study focuses primarily on predictors of change in these components of functioning, the trajectories of functional change, the interrelationships of change in multiple domains, and on the consequences of change in functioning in terms of older persons' contributions to society, their adjustment and their need for care. In addition, detailed information has been collected in specific sub-samples, including the course of depression (1992-1999) and falls and osteoporotic fractures (1995-1999).

The LASA cohort is based on a random sample drawn from three culturally distinct geographical areas in the west, north-east, and south of the Netherlands, and weighted according to expected mortality within each sex and age group. At baseline in 1992/93, LASA included 3,107 subjects aged 55-85 years drawn from the sample of the NESTOR project (described elsewhere in this report). The LASA baseline was taken about 11 months after the NESTOR survey with subsequent waves every three years. Self-reported data on chronic diseases and depressive symptoms and performance tests of physical ability were collected by personal interviews. Clinical assessments and bio-assays were taken by a nurse in a separate medical interview. Mortality was ascertained two years after baseline.

Findings from the LASA data have been published in several books and research journals including:

Deeg, D. J. H. and M. Westendorp de Serriere (eds). 1992-93. *Autonomy and Well-being in the Aging Population: Report from the Longitudinal Aging Study*, Amsterdam

Deeg, D. J. H., D. M. W. Kriegsman and A.T.F. Beekman. 1995. "Association of Chronic Diseases and Depression with Physical Test Performance and Mortality", presented at the III European Congress of Gerontology, Amsterdam.

7.1.2 EUROPEAN LONGITUDINAL STUDY ON AGEING (ELSA)
Eino Heikkinen, Principal Investigator
The Finnish Centre of Interdisciplinary Gerontology, University of Jyväskylä, Jyväskylä, Finland
Dates: 1979 - 1996

The European Longitudinal Study on Ageing (ELSA) is a major comparative research project that uses a panel, cohort comparative and cross-cultural setting to examine the changing patterns of health, functional ability, life situation, way of life, and use of services of the elderly. The original project, "The Eleven Countries Study on Health Care of the

Elderly", was initiated by the WHO Regional Office for Europe. The first stage of the study was carried out in 1979-80 in the form of an epidemiological survey among representative population samples in 16 areas of various European countries. Altogether 17,000 persons took part in the interviews. In order to examine ageing processes and cohort differences, a follow-up study was conducted by seven of the study centres (Bialystok, Poland; Berlin, Germany; Brussels, Belgium; Florence, Italy; Athens, Greece; Kiev, Ukraine; Tampere, Finland).

The baseline survey of men and women in six five-year age groups from age 60-89 years at interview was conducted in 1979-80. Altogether 15 centres from Europe and one from Kuwait participated the baseline study. Comparable instruments were used across research sites. Each centre aimed to select at least 100 individuals of each 5-year age group from 60 to 89 years of age. To help understand the potential differences in the use of services between the study areas it was agreed to make an inventory of local service systems.

The longitudinal study was put into effect in 1986-90, approximately 8 to 10 years after the baseline study. Seven of the original study areas participated: Berlin (West), Germany; Bialystok, Poland; Brussels, Belgium; Florence, Italy; rural Greece; Kiev, Ukraine; and Tampere, Finland. Each of the centres carried out at least one of the four components: 1) follow-up of the original cross-sectional sample; 2) mortality study; 3) new cross-sectional survey (for age cohort comparison: 60-64 and 65-69 years old men and women in 1979 and 1989); and 4) service inventory (changes in the health service systems). In the longitudinal setting, the analyses have mainly concentrated on changes in, and predictors of, health and functional ability as well as on changes and cultural differences in social contacts and ways of life.

7.1.3 GRONINGEN LONGITUDINAL AGING STUDY (GLAS)
Johan Ormel, Principal Investigator
School of Medicine, University of Groningen, Groningen, The Netherlands
Dates: 1993 - 1997 (first phase)

The purpose of this project is to evaluate the influence of psychosocial factors on health-related quality of life, and to compare subjective and performance-based tests of functioning at different levels. This project seeks to understand the extent to which functional status, well-being, attitudes about care arrangements, and the utilisation of care among elderly people are related and how psychosocial, environmental, and life-style and behavioural factors influence these interrelationships.

The objectives of the study are addressed by the combination of a baseline cross-sectional study of 5,279 people 57 years of age and older , and a longitudinal follow-up of 753 frail elderly selected out of the baseline sample followed annually for three years. A prospective cohort study will be conducted among those subjects who experience falls with complications, hip fractures, myocardial infarction, heart failure, depression, acute hospital admission or death of spouse in the three years following the baseline assessment. A fitness sub-study also will be conducted among a random sample of 624 participants from the baseline population to examine the relationship between self-reported functional status and a limited set of performance-based capacity tests.

7.1.4 OLDEST-OLD MORTALITY--DEMOGRAPHIC MODELS AND ANALYSES
James Vaupel, Principal Investigator
Odense University, Odense, Denmark and Duke University, Durham, NC, USA
Dates: 1993 - ongoing

This research project focuses four main issues concerning trajectories of mortality at advanced ages: (1) the environmental and genetic plasticity of mortality rates; (2) the deceleration of mortality with age; (3) the interrelationship between disability and mortality; and (4) male-female differences. In support of these goals, data on oldest-old mortality rates and various covariates (such as causes of death and functioning) for various populations, including males and females in the United States and 27 other countries in recent decades, MZ twins and both same-sex and different-sex DZ twins born in Denmark between 1870 and 1930, and three related fruit-fly species, as well as inbred lines of Drosophila are being collected, verified, standardized, and provided for public use to researchers.

This project also will develop and use demographic and statistical methods (including life-table, extinct-cohort, smoothing, and survival-analysis methods, lexis-map methods; adaptations of methods of quantitative trait locus analysis and GoM models) to summarise the data and describe trajectories of mortality at advanced ages, including analysis of how mortality rates change with age, over time, for successive birth cohorts, across different countries, across different areas of the United States, for males vs. females, for different causes of death (for Danish twins), at different ADL levels, for different species, for different genotypes, and for population (of Drosophila) that share different chromosomal regions (quantitative trait loci). Alternative theory-based models will be developed that incorporate biological knowledge and fit them to the data to gain an understanding of ageing and mortality. These models will include genetic and environmental factors, mortality trajectories for individuals, and mortality selection in heterogeneous populations.

The data collected by this project are archived at the Odense University Medical School in the Archive of Population Data on Aging and are available, with permission of the investigator, from the Danish Data Archives. A description of the Odense Archive of Mortality data has been published in:

Kannisto, Väinö. 1994. *Development of oldest-old mortality, 1950-1990: evidence from 28 developed countries*. Odense, Denmark: Odense University Press.

Findings from these studies also have been published in a large number of books and research journals and include:

Manton, Kenneth G. and James W. Vaupel. 1995. "Survival after the age of 80 in the United States, Sweden, France, England, and Japan". *New England Journal of Medicine*, 333(18):1232-5.

Herskind, A. M., M. McGue, I. A. Iachine, N. Holm, T. I. Sorensen, B. Harvald and J. W. Vaupel. 1996. "Untangling genetic influences on smoking, body mass index and longevity: a multivariate study of 2464 Danish twins followed for 28 years." *Human Genetics*, 98(4):467-75.

Carey, James R., Pablo Liedo and James W. Vaupel. 1995. "Mortality dynamics of density in the Mediterranean fruit fly". *Experimental Gerontology*, 30(6):605-29.

7.1.5 ITALIAN LONGITUDINAL STUDY ON AGING (ILSA)
Luigi A. Amaducci and Stefania Maggi, Principal Investigators
University of Florence, Florence, Italy
Dates: 1992 - ongoing

The Italian Longitudinal Study on Aging (ILSA) is a multi-centre project designed to study age-related diseases and physiologic and functional changes resulting from the ageing of the cardiovascular, endocrine, metabolic and nervous systems in a random sample of 5,632 older Italians, aged 64-84 years, stratified by age and sex, living in the study area on March 1, 1992. The study has two components: first, a two-phase survey, with a screening phase that includes a personal interview, a physician examination, laboratory and diagnostic tests. The baseline examination ascertains the prevalence of specific diseases and measures the exposure to potential risk factors. Risk factors include education, occupation, social network, smoking and alcohol use, nutrition, and biological factors. Subjects suspected of having one of the diseases of interest (angina, myocardial infarction, hypertension, congestive heart failure, arrythmia, peripheral arteriopathy, diabetes, impaired glucose tolerance, disthyroidisms, dementia, parkinsonism, stroke, peripheral neuropathies) during this phase are sent for clinical assessment and differential diagnosis by a specialist (geriatrician or neurologist) who will search for specific disorders within a syndrome. Incident and recurrent cases of non-fatal and fatal diseases in the sample are identified through a hospital discharge survey and a mortality survey, performed two years after the prevalence survey, and through the complete re-interview and clinical examination, administered every three years to all participants.

The collected information is used to: assess prevalence rates for the diseases of interest; establish comparisons across the eight centres involved in the study and with those obtained in other studies in Italy and in other countries; establish the distribution of the potential social, behavioural, environmental, and economic risk factors in the older population and assess incidence rates of both first and recurrent diseases and how they differ across the eight centres. The project also seeks to identify the total and cause-specific mortality rates and the hospitalisation rates in this cohort and the physiologic and functional changes related to the ageing process and to the presence of diseases.

A description of the survey design and methodology may be found in

> Maggi, Stefania, S. M. Zucchetto, F. Grigoletto, C. M. Baldereschi, L. E. Scarpini, G. Scarlato and L. Amaducci. 1994. "The Italian Longitudinal Study on Aging (ILSA): design and methods". *Aging*, 6(6):464-73.

Preliminary findings have been published in:

> Maggi, Stefania. 1995. *Chronic conditions and cause-specific mortality rates in older Italians*, National Research Council: Firenze, Italy

> Langlois, J.A., S. Maggi, E.M. Simonsick, et al. 1996. "Self-Report of Difficulty in Performing Functional Activities Identifies a Broad Range of Disability in Old Age". *Journal of the American Geriatrics Society*, 44(12):1421-8

7.1.6 AMSTERDAM STUDY OF THE ELDERLY (AMSTEL)
Cees Jonker, Principal Investigator
Vrije Universiteit, Amsterdam, The Netherlands
Dates: 1989 - 1994

The Amsterdam Study of the Elderly (Amstel) was a longitudinal study of the development of psychopathology that began in 1990. The central question focused on the course of cognitive decline in the elderly. The main objective of the study was to improve the early diagnosis of dementia, in particular of Alzheimer's disease. Several cognitive screening instruments (including the Mini-Mental State) were used, as well as measurements of education, pre-morbid intelligence (NART) and relevant measures for socio-economic and biological function. Scales for anxiety and depression, derived from the Geriatric Mental State Schedule (GMS) were included in the baseline measurement.

The baseline was conducted with an initial sample of 4,051 persons aged between 65-84 living in the greater Amsterdam region. These respondents were re-interviewed after four years with the same questionnaire. In addition, a cohort of 511 subjects was selected from the baseline population, based on the severity of cognitive impairment. This cohort was followed annually until 1995. The aim of this part of the study was to record extensive cognitive measures in order to diagnose the type and severity of dementia and psychiatric disorders in the cohort. Published results include:

Jonker, C. and C. Hooyer. 1990. "The Amstel project: design and first findings. The course of mild cognitive impairment of the aged; a longitudinal 4-year study". *Psychiatric Journal of the University of Ottawa*, 15(4):207-11,.

Walter-Launer, L. J., A. W. Wind and D. J. Deeg. 1995. "Nonresponse pattern and bias in a community-based cross-sectional study of cognitive functioning among the elderly". *American Journal of Epidemiology*, 139(8):803-12

7.1.7 CROSS-SECTIONAL AND LONGITUDINAL AGEING STUDY (CALAS)
Baruch Modan, Principal Investigator
The Chaim Sheba Medical Center, Tel-Hashomer, Israel
Dates: 1988 - ongoing

The main objective of this project is to define risk factors for general health and well-being in later life on the basis of social and clinical parameters. The basic question is the extent to which there are early life predictors of a long-term trajectory of health and functioning in later life and the extent to which these trajectories are triggered by specific events.

A corollary objective is assessing changes in the natural course disease conditions affecting the older population in Israel, and the effect of changes in life style risk factors on these changes. Other questions being addressed include: (1) Whether the elderly from different ethnic groups in Israel (European/American, Asian/African, Israeli born) have different patterns of mortality, institutionalisation, and functional impairment; (2) The extent to which the supportive environment of the kibbutz contributes to a decrease in mortality, institutionalisation, and functional impairment; and (3) whether older holocaust survivors have lower age-specific rates of mortality, institutionalisation, and functional impairment than those who left Europe before 1939

In 1989, a baseline assessment of health and functional status, health-care utilisation, subjective well-being, and socio-familial networks in a multi-cultural framework was conducted. The random stratified sample consisted of 2,891 Jewish subjects aged 75 and over chosen from the Central Population Register. A total of 1820 (76%) of the 75-94 age group were interviewed during 1989-1992. In addition, all 652 kibbutz residents in the country aged 85+ and a sample of 674 residents aged 75-84 were similarly studied. The original members of the baseline study were located and they or their survivors were re-interviewed three to five years after the original interview. In the follow-up survey an additional cognitive exam (Folstein) and a 24-hour dietary recall interview were added.

Project results have been presented in:

> Walter-Ginzburg A., T. Blumstein, J. Guralnik, Z. Fuchs, Z. Shapira and B. Modan. 1995. " Assistance with personal care activities among the oldest-old Jews in the CALAS study in Israel", presented at the III European Congress of Gerontology, Amsterdam, 30 August - 2 September 1995.

7.1.8 SATSA - THE SWEDISH ADOPTION/TWIN STUDY OF AGEING
Nancy Pedersen, Paul Lichtenstein, Ulf de Faire, Principal Investigators
Karolinska Institutet, Stockholm, Sweden
Dates: 1984-Ongoing

The Swedish Adoption/Twin Study of Ageing (SATSA) was initiated to examine the relative importance of genetic and environmental factors for individual differences in ageing. SATSA began in 1984 and is comprised of several longitudinal components. A comprehensive questionnaire was sent in the first component to all twins separated at an early age and reared apart and a control sample of twins reared together from the Swedish Twin Registry. The Swedish Twin Registry was established in 1961. It includes an old cohort, comprised of 10,945 pairs of same-sex twins born between 1886 and 1925, and a middle cohort comprised of approximately 50,000 pairs of same-sex and mixed-sex twins born 1926 through 1967, and a young cohort of approximately 25,000 pairs born since 1967. The twin registry is matched regularly to sources of vital statistics in Sweden. Plans exist to expand the registry by contacting all 116,000 living individuals for screening of diseases and collection of blood samples.

The SATSA questionnaire included items concerning work environment, health status, health-related behaviours (e.g. alcohol, tobacco, and dietary habits), and attitude and personality measures. The questionnaire phase is repeated every third year: Thus far more than 2,000 twins have responded to questionnaires sent in 1984, 1987, 1990 and 1993. In the second component a subsample of approximately 150 twin pairs reared apart and 150 twin pairs reared together have participated in three waves of in-person testing including general health, functional capacity, cognitive abilities, and memory.

Among the studies being conducted with these data are: environmental factors for cardiovascular disease; dementia in Swedish twins; sex differences in health and ageing; genetic influences on affective disorders; changes in functional abilities in relationship to well-being in the oldest-old; and genetic and environmental effects on longevity.

Publications include:

> Pederson, N. L., P. Lichtenstein, U. D. Faire, A. Ahlbom, B. Floderus and M. Svartengren. 1996. "En (inter)nationell resurs. Svenskt tvillingregister ger upplysning om miljons och arvets betydelse vid sjukdom. [An (inter)national

resource. The Swedish registry on twins informs on the role of environment and heredity in diseases]". *Lakartidningen*, 93(12):1127-30, March 20, 1996.

Gatz, Margaret, Nancy L. Pederson, Robert Plomi and John R. Nesselroade. 1992. "Importance of shared genes and shared environments for symptoms of depression in older adults". *Journal of Abnormal Psychology*, Vol 101(4) 701-708.

Nikolic, Jovanka and Eileen Crimmins. 1995. "Determinants of changes in Health and Physical Functioning Among a Sample of Older Swedes", paper presented at the 8th International Meeting of REVES, Chicago, USA, October 1995.

7.1.9 RESTRICTION IN DAILY LIVING ACTIVITY AMONG ELDERLY
Margareta N. Mutafova, Principal Investigator
Medical University, Sofia, Bulgaria
Dates: 1992 - 1995

The primary purpose of this project was to collect the information necessary to calculate estimates of healthy and disabled life expectancy for the Bulgarian population. A health interview survey was conducted among people 60 years and older. The questionnaire used in this study was constructed according to the recommendation of the WHO concerning common methods and instruments for health interview surveys. Functional status was measured by the personal assessment of independence or dependence in carrying out the basic activities of daily living. Data for long-term disability were obtained from a 10-item indicator concerning locomotion, transfer, dressing, washing, feeding, toilette, continence, hearing and seeing. Data to determine handicaps come from another set of questions concerning mobility. Assessment of perceived health also was obtained.

The investigation was carried out among non-institutionalised persons aged 60 years and over in a middle-sized town in Bulgaria in December 1992, and after 12 months all the people were re-interviewed. In the first phase, interviews were obtained from 1,390 persons representing about 50 percent of all people in this age group in the town. By the end of 1993, personal interviews had been conducted with 1,242 older respondents.

7.1.10 ELDERLY AGED 60 AND OVER IN HOUSEHOLDS IN ISRAEL
Eitan Sabatello and Dorith Tal, Principal Investigators
Central Bureau of Statistics, Jerusalem, Israel
Dates: 1996 - 1997

The main objectives of this project are to update and extend the Elderly National Survey carried out in 1985 to establish a longitudinal database on ageing in Israel. Approximately 5,000 persons aged 60 and over in 3,800 households were surveyed in 1997. Where possible, individual records were matched with the 1985 survey. The data therefore include both cross-sectional as well as some longitudinal data. Among the topics included in the survey were: self-assessed health perception; hearing ability, vision, physical mobility, morbidity; use of health services, ADL and IADL, social and family support and networks, voluntary activities, leisure activities; past and present employment, income sources, and housing conditions. Analysis will include studies of the trajectories of health and social changes over the 12 years between the two surveys; and a comparative study of the elderly in Israel with those in other western countries.

7.1.11 THE SWEDISH PANEL STUDY OF LIVING CONDITIONS OF THE OLDEST OLD (SWEOLD).

Mats Thorslund, Principal Investigator.
Stockholm University, Stockholm, Sweden.
Dates: February 1992 - ongoing

This study aims to describe the living conditions and health of the oldest-old and to examine differences between groups, according to such characteristics as social class, gender, age and birth cohort. A second goal is to examine the subjects' living conditions and health in old age in relation to data gathered 24 years earlier on the same respondents.

SWEOLD originated in the 1968 Level of Living Survey, a nationally representative sample of 6,000 persons aged 16 to 75. The interview covered demographic variables, living conditions, use of health and social services, working conditions, economy, health, and social situation. The data was supplemented with register data, such as number of sick days, income, and social benefits. In 1992, respondents who were over 75 were traced and re-interviewed. Of 1,936 possible respondents, 563 were still alive and living in Sweden. Of these, a total of 537 persons were interviewed. Proxy interviews were carried out for those persons (12.4%) who could not be interviewed directly. The interview included several of the items included in the original Level of Living Survey, as well as questions on health, health care utilisation, use of medicines, self rated health, cognitive and physical function (peak expiratory flow, ADL and performance tests), and social contacts. For deceased persons, date and cause of death are available.

Findings from the project have been reported in:

> Thorslund, Mats and Olle Lundberg. 1994. "Health and Inequalities Among the Oldest-Old". *Journal of Aging and Health*, 6(1):51-69.

7.1.12 AGING IN LEGANÉS
Maria-Victoria Zunzunegui, Principal Investigator
Escuela Andaluza de Salud Pública, Madrid, Spain
Dates: 1993 - 2001

The purpose of this project is to provide information on ageing in a Spanish community that can be used by public authorities to develop guidelines for long-term care policies that promote autonomy of the elderly and their ability to dwell in the community. The focus is on the influence of social support on the evolution of health status and functional capacity, the use of health and social services, institutionalisation, and mortality. These interrelationships are studied longitudinally to develop causal inferences.

The study utilises a longitudinal, age-period-cohort design. The final sample of 1,284 persons in Wave I represents the community dwelling population aged 65 or over in the city of Leganés. Five waves of data collection are being undertaken every two years beginning in 1993. On each of these occasions, the sample will be refreshed to include those who aged into the 65-66 year age group. Data were collected during two home visits through personal interviews with a structured questionnaire and a physical examination conducted by a doctor. Information was gathered on health, use of services, socio-economic conditions, and social support, disability, memory, accidents, and lifestyles. The physical examination included blood pressure, hearing and vision exams and a dental exam.

Findings from the research are reported in:

Béland, François and Victoria Zunzunegui. 1995. "La Ayuda Recibida por las Personas Mayores". *Revista de Gerontologia*, 5(4):294-308.

Béland, François and Victoria Zunzunegui. 1995. "El Perfil de las Incapacidades Funcionales en las Personas Mayores". *Revista de Gerontologia*, 5(4):232-244.

Béland, François and Victoria Zunzunegui. 1995. "La Salud y las Incapacidades Funcionales: Elaboración de un Modelo Causal". *Revista de Gerontologia*, 5(4):259-273.

7.1.13 NATIONAL-ETHNIC PECULIARITIES OF AGEING IN UKRAINE
Svetlana Kuznetsova, Principal Investigator
Institute of Gerontology, Academy of Medical Sciences, Kiev, Ukraine
Dates: Ongoing

The main purpose of this project is to study the health-related changes with age in different ethnic groups in the Ukraine and to elucidate the role of socio-economic and biological factors in the development of age-related pathology. The study also involves study of the role of social and environmental factors in the distribution of regional and ethnic differences in the rate of cardiovascular diseases and the pathologies of the nervous system. Ethnic groups being studied include Russians, Ukrainians, Tatars, Jews, and Bielorussians.

The project was designed as an epidemiological longitudinal study. The sample included 4,000 subjects aged 60 and older in rural regions of South Ukraine (Crimea) and Western Ukraine. The research includes an interview survey concerning health, social, and economic factors, and a doctor's clinical assessment of health including electro-cardiogram, electro-encephalogram, blood lipid and lipoproteins and other blood characteristics. The data being collected also includes regional demographic information and environmental data (comprising standard analysis of water, air, soil, heavy metals and pesticides), information on health behaviours including nutrition, employment, family structure, and ethnic traditions. The data on the first, cross-sectional stage of study have already been collected and analysed.

7.1.14 PAQUID. Study of Normal And Pathological Aging
Jean Francois Dartigues, Principal Investigator
INSERM, Université de Bordeaux, France
Dates: 1988 - Ongoing

The PAQUID ("QUID" sur les Personnes Agées) Research Program is a prospective cohort study of mental and physical aging that evaluates social environment, health status, cognitive functioning and depressive symptoms in a representative random sample of 4,000 subjects aged 65 years and older, in two geographical areas of South-Western France (Gironde and Dordogne). One of the major goals of the PAQUID Research Program is to determine the incidence, risk factors and preclinical manifestations of Senile Dementia of the Alzheimer's Type. The second goal of PAQUID is to describe the disability process after the age of 65, and to identify the major risk factors and consequences as measured by institutionalization and mortality. Of particular interest is the relationship between physical, cognitive, depressive and social components of dependence. Published results include:

Dartigues, J. F., P. Barberger-Gateau, M. Gagnon, D. Commenges, A. Alpérovitch, A. Decamps and R. Salamon. 1991. "Paquid: étude épidémiologique du vieillissement normal et pathologique". *Revue Gériatrique,* 16:5-15.

Barberger-Gateau, P., A. Chaslerie, J. F. Dartigues, D. Commenges, M. Gagnon and R. Salamon. 1992. "Health Measures Correlates in a French Elderly Community Population: the PAQUID Study". *Journal of Gerontology: Social Sciences*, 47:88-95.

Launer, L.J., C. Brayne, J. F. Dartigues and A. Hofman. 1992. "European studies on the incidence of dementing diseases". *Neuroepidemiology,* 11 (Suppl. 1):1-122.

7.1.15 THE NOTTINGHAM LONGITUDINAL STUDY OF ACTIVITY AND AGEING (NLSAA)

Kevin Morgan, Principal Investigator
University of Nottingham, Nottingham, United Kingdom
Dates: 1985 - 1996

The NLSAA was a longitudinal study of elderly people living at home. It was designed to assess the contribution of lifestyle and customary physical activity in promoting and maintaining mental health and psychological well-being in later life, when controlling for social, domestic, economic, functional and clinical status. The baseline survey of 1,299 persons aged 65 and older was conducted in 1985 in Nottinghamshire. Information on mortality within the baseline sample was recorded, and follow-up surveys of all eligible survivors were conducted between May 1989 and September 1993. Information collected includes household structure, health and mobility, smoking and health behaviours, self-assessed health, life satisfaction, morale and depression, and the majority of questions on activities: social, work, household, and leisure. Published results include:

Ebrahim et al. 1988. "Causes of ill-health among a random sample of old and very old people: possibilities for prevention". *Journal of the Royal College of Physicians of London,* 22:105-107.

Morgan et al. 1991. "Customary physical activity, psychological well-being and successful ageing". *Ageing and Society*, 11(4): 399-416

7.1.16 MELTON MOWBRAY AGEING PROJECT

Carol Jagger, Principal Investigator.
University of Leicester, Leicester, United Kingdom
Dates: 1981 - 1997

This project is a longitudinal study of the physical and mental health and social status of older people and their use of health-care services. The ongoing collection of mortality data also has enabled investigation of the predictors of survival and estimation of healthy life expectancy. The data collection includes two cross-sectional surveys (1981 and 1988) and an intermediate follow-up (1985) of all patients aged 75 years and over who were registered with a large medical practice in Leicestershire, England. The total sample size was 1,203 in

1981 and 1,579 in 1988. Community and institutional residents were included in both cohorts and follow-ups. All three survey instruments covered demographic information, physical and mental functioning, and the use of health and social services. A detailed psychiatric interview was conducted on a those with low scores on the Mini-Mental State Examination (MMSE) for clinical evaluation of dementia (including subtypes). Results from this project have been disseminated widely in research journals and focus on the investigation of prevalence and risk factors for medical conditions such as dementia, diabetes, cataract, incontinence and hypertension. The data also have been used to examine mortality risks from widowhood and visual impairment, and trajectories of functional capacity. Some recent Publications include:

> Jagger, C., M. Clarke and S. J. Clarke. 1991. "Getting older, feeling younger: the changing health profile of the elderly". *International Journal of Epidemiology,* 20:234-238.

> Jagger C. and C. J. Sutton. 1991. "Death after marital bereavement is the risk increased?". *Statistics in Medicine,* 10:395-404.

> Jagger C., M. Clarke, J. Anderson and T. Battcock. 1992. "Misclassification of dementia by the mini mental state examination are education and social class the only factors?". *Age and Ageing ,* 21:404-11.

> Jagger, C., N. A. Spiers and M. Clarke 1993. "Factors associated with decline in function, institutionalisation & mortality in the elderly". *Age and Ageing,* 22:190-7.

Further information about the projects may be found on the World Wide Web at http://www.prw.le.ac.uk/ dept/research/melton/

7.1.17 AGEING IN AN EPIDEMIOLOGICAL-ECOLOGICAL CONTEXT. A FIVE-YEAR FOLLOW-UP STUDY OF 75-YEAR-OLD PEOPLE LIVING IN THREE NORDIC LOCALITIES (NORA)
Eino M. Heikkinen, Principal Investigator.
University of Jyväskylä, Jyväskylä, Finland
Dates: 1989 - 1999

This project was undertaken to compare functional capacity and health among elderly people living in three different Nordic urban localities, and to study the predictors of observed functional capacity and population differences.

Between 1989 and 1991, a sample of 1,388 persons aged 75 and over was drawn in cities in Denmark, Finland, and Sweden. The final sample sizes were 388 in Jyväskylä; 450 in Göteborg; and 550 in Glostrup. Participants were evaluated with performance tests in laboratory settings for functional capacity and health, using techniques comparable to earlier studies in Glostrup, Gothenburg, and Jyväskylä. Physical tests included cholesterol scores and hormone levels, anthropometric assessments, aerobic power, strength, visual acuity, and audiometry, neuro-psycological and cognitive tests, among others. Subjects also provided health, functioning, and social, and demographic information in standardized questionnaires. A detailed description of the project may be found in:

> Schroll, M., B. Steen, S. Berg, E. Heikkinen and A. Vidik. 1993. "NORA - Nordic Research on Ageing: Functional capacity of 75 Year Old Men and Women in Three Nordic Localities". *Danish Medical Bulletin,* 40:618-624.

7.1.18 CHANGES IN ELDERLY MORTALITY AND PROJECTIONS OF THE ELDERLY POPULATION OF ITALY
Frank Heins, Principal Investigator
Institute of Population Research, National Research Council, Rome, Italy
Dates: 1995 - ongoing

The main purpose of this project is to analyse the geographic differences and trends in elderly mortality, to formulate alternative future trends in elderly mortality and to establish population projections. To estimate the future trends in ageing this research project will analyse recent trends in geographic differences in elderly mortality. Based on this analysis, investigators will forecast mortality - specifically elderly mortality - and develop various scenarios regarding mortality trends for the next 10 to 20 years in the major regions of Italy. Based on these different scenarios of elderly mortality, regional population projections with special regard toward population ageing will be established.

7.1.19 ALTERNATIVE POPULATION PROJECTIONS FOR MAJOR WORLD REGIONS.
Wolfgang Lutz, Principal investigator
International Institute for Applied Systems Analysis (IIASA), Laxenburg, Austria
Dates: 1993 - 1997

This project will produce country-specific alternative population scenarios for twelve regions of the world, including Europe. These alternative population scenarios are intended to be contrasted with existing EUROSTAT and UN Population Projections. They consider several different mortality and fertility scenarios from the most likely to the most extreme. Particular attention has been paid to variations in older-adult mortality patterns. Information about the project may be obtained on the internet at the following site: http://www.iiasa.ac.at/Research/POP/docs/Population_Projections_Results.html

Results have been published in:

> Lutz, Wolfgang (ed.). 1996. *The Future Population of the World: What Can We Assume Today? (Updated and Revised Edition)*. Earthscan Publications Ltd., London, UK.

> Lutz, Wolfgang, W. Sanderson and S. Scherbov, 1995. *Probabilistic Population Projections Based on Expert Opinion*, WP-95-123, International Institute for Applied Systems Analysis, Laxenburg, Austria.

7.1.20 SENECA: SURVEY IN EUROPE ON NUTRITION OF THE ELDERLY, A CONCERTED ACTION.
Wija Van Staveren, Principal Investigator
Wageningen Agricultural University, Wageningen, The Netherlands
Dates: 1987 - 1997

This is a longitudinal study to explore dietary and lifestyle patterns of elderly people across Europe in relation to their health and functioning. The study included a survey, dietary interview, anthropometric measurements, blood biochemistries, non-responders-study, MMSE, GDS, and physical performance tests. Baseline interviews were conducted in 1988 and follow-up measurement in 1993 at sites in 19 European countries and the United States:

The sample comprised 2,600 persons aged 70-75 across all sites at initial interview in 1988. This project is being funded by the European Union as a focus for its program of concerted action on gerontology. Some findings have been published in:

de Groot, L., J. Hautvast and W. van Staveren. 1992. "Nutrition and the Health of Elderly People in Europe: The EURONUT-SENECA Study". *Nutrition Reviews*, (50)7:185-194.

7.1.21 EUGERON AND EXCELSA: AGEING, HEALTH AND COMPETENCE.

Johannes J. Schroots, Principal Investigator
European Research Institute on Health and Aging, University of Amsterdam, Amsterdam, The Netherlands
Dates: EuGeron - 1994 - 1997
**   EXCELSA - 1997 - ongoing.**

The general objective of EuGeron is to develop a knowledge base about the conditions of health and functioning that promote or inhibit independent living in relation to age. This knowledge is necessary to develop realistic public policies with regard to ageing in different geographic and socio-economic European settings. The original research program is designed as a multicentre study representing combined cross-sectional, longitudinal and intervention studies. The EuGeron project, in which 14 EU member states and three Eastern European countries are collaborating began in May 1994. Within the EuGeron project, preparations are being made for multidisciplinary and multicentric data collection in the Cross-European Longitudinal Study of Ageing (EXCELSA). This project is being funded by the European Union as a focus for its program of concerted action on gerontology.

The goal of the EXCELSA project is to study the factors which contribute to the maintenance of health and functioning in older persons using a longitudinal study design, relying on highly structured and standardized assessments and developing similar probability based sampling strategies across countries leading to the enrolment of comparable cohorts of participants. The major goal is to describe the variability and heterogeneity in socio-economic, physical, and mental function occuring in different cultures under varying circumstances.

The EXCELSA surveys planned for 1998 in 17 countries (Austria, Belgium, Denmark, Finland, France, Germany, Greece, Italy, Lithuania, Luxembourg, The Netherlands, Poland, Portugal, Spain, Sweden, United Kingdom, Ukraine). A representative community-based sample of about 3,000 individuals, aged 30-85 will be interviewed in the baseline wave for each participating country.

7.1.22 LUND 80+: A LONGITUDINAL, SEQUENTIAL STUDY OF 80 YEAR-OLDS AND OLDER IN SWEDEN.

Torbjörn F. Svensson, Principal Investigator
Gerontology Research Center, Lund, Sweden
Dates: 1988 - 2009

The main purpose of this project is study the medical, psychological and social aspects of the ageing process among the oldest old (aged 80 years and over). In particular, the project examines aspects of ageing as defined by ecological models of ageing. To separate age, period, and cohort effects, the study incorporates both longitudinal and cohort sequential designs.. A secondary project goal is to evaluate the effect of the yearly visit to the local health station that is part of the first examination. The major areas of ageing being studied include psychological factors related to cognition, personality, adaptation and coping strategies. The social conditions, social networks, medical conditions and morbidity are all under study.

The first cohort (born 1908) was examined first in 1988. These persons are re-examined annually. A new cohort will be admitted every fifth year for 20 years, and re-examined every five years. The total number of participants for the first year was 211. In subsequent waves, the number of survivors was 148, 120, 91, 69, and 46 respectively. Project results have been reported in:

Svensson, T., O. Dehlin, B. Hagberg and G. Samuelsson. 1993. The Lund 80+ study: Some general findings. in J. J. F. Schroots (ed.), *Aging, health and competence. The next generation of longitudinal research*. Amsterdam: Elsevier Science Publishers.

Svensson, T., O. Dehlin, B. Hagberg and G. Samuelsson. 1989. Lund 80+: En longitudinell studie med sekvensiell design av personer över 80 år i Lund. Pilotstudie. *Gerontologiskt Centrum*, III:2, 1989

Jensen, E., R. Liang, O. Dehlin, B. Hagberg, G. Samuelsson and T. Svensson. The relationships between laboratory values and quality of life in an 80-year-old population. *Scandinavian Journal of Primary Health Care*.

7.1.23   REYKJAVIK 80+: A LONGITUDINAL STUDY OF 80 YEAR-OLDS AND OLDER IN ICELAND
Jón Jónsson, Principal Investigator
Reykjavik, Iceland
Dates: 1993-ongoing

Launched in 1993, the Reykjavik 80+ study is, based on and is an extension of the Lund 80+ study. The study population comprised all of the 437 residents of Reykjavik born in 1913. A total of 282 individuals, of whom 103 (37%) were males and 179 (63%) were females, took part in the first wave of the study. This was an overall response rate of 64.5% which is identical to that first cohort in Lund 80+ study. See the entry for Lund for further information on the study design.

7.1.24 DEVELOPMENTS IN HEALTH EXPECTANCY IN DENMARK
Henrik Brønnum-Hansen, Principal Investigator
The Danish Institute for Clinical Epidemiology, Copenhagen, Denmark
Dates: 1995 - 1996

The objective of this project is to calculate a time series of life expectancy and healthy life expectancy estimates for the adult Danish population for the period 1987 to 1994. Nationally representative random samples of Danish adults aged 16 years or older were interviewed in 1986-87, 1990-91, and 1994 to establish prevalence estimates of disability and illness. These estimates are combined with life tables for the corresponding years to calculate prevalence based measures of healthy life expectancy using the Sullivan method.

7.1.25   BIOLOGICAL, CLINICAL, MORPHOLOGICAL AND PERSONALITY PARAMETERS OF LONGEVITY.
Iván László, Principal Investigator
Semmelweis University of Medicine, Budapest, Hungary
Dates: 1995 - 1997

This is a longitudinal study of two groups of individuals aged 60 and over selected from the patients of the Clinical Department and the Geriatric Risk-Screening Clinic of the Gerontology Centre of the Semmelweis University of Medicine, Budapest. Based on the European Senior Protocol, the study will establish one low risk and one high risk group. Individuals of both groups will be entered in the "follow-up geriatric program" of the Centre. The topics of the "follow-up geriatric program" are as follows: (1) life style, life motivation and activities; (2) self estimation with personality structure analysis; (3) nutritional habits; and (4) biological and psychological factors (dehydroepiandosterone, substances acting against free radicals, selective light therapeutic measures, etc.). Subjects will be examined for age-related biological, neuropsychiatric and pathological changes and their influence on longevity.

7.1.26 CARDIAC FAILURE IN ELDERLY OF DICOMANO (I CARE DICOMANO)
Giulio Masotti, Principal Investigator
Department of Gerontology and Geriatric Medicine, University of Florence, Italy
Dates: 1989 - 1995

This project encompasses a series of cross-sectional and longitudinal epidemiological studies of the community-dwelling elderly population of Dicomano in Italy. It is primarily concerned with validating the diagnosis of cardiac failure at the epidemiological level in older subjects. Cardiac failure in the elderly may be reported with atypical symptoms, therefore the clinical, pathophysiological and functional features of cardiac failure in elderly populations need to be more accurately investigated. The questions addressed by the I CARe Dicomano project include validating the criteria commonly used for the diagnosis of cardiac failure in a home-dwelling elderly population and developing a reliable and appropriate cluster of diagnostic criteria to be used prospectively in new epidemiological surveys. The project also seeks to document the prevalence of the different pathophysiological forms (i.e. systolic vs. diastolic dysfunction) of cardiac failure in an elderly population and to identify risk factors for cardiac failure in its different forms. The final goal of the project is to understand the impact of cardiac failure on the overall health status and the general performance of older persons, and the role of co-morbidity in modifying the effect of cardiac failure on disability.

The study was designed in 1989 as a multidimensional survey of the general state of health of the elderly (65+ years) population residing in Dicomano (Florence, Italy). In 1995, a follow-up study of the survivors of the 1989 cohort was conducted and a new cross-sectional study enrolled those who had aged into to the sample during the six-year interval. This study involves 899 subjects aged 65 or older. The I CARe project was designed to gather the same information as in 1989, plus an extensive non-invasive diagnostic evaluation (ECG, echocardiography, Doppler vascular exam, chest x-ray, spirometry), performance measures and ADL/IADL estimates of physical functioning, information on comorbidity, Geriatric Depression Scale profiles, and social conditions and interactions.

7.2 ECONOMIC

7.2.1 ECONOMIC ASPECTS OF AGEING (CERRA)
Jules Theeuwes, Principal Investigator
Leiden University, Leiden, The Netherlands
Dates: 1 October 1992 - 1 October 1996

The main objectives of this project are to construct a longitudinal dataset of Dutch elderly that contains information on retirement behaviour, health and income dynamics, and labour force participation and retirement behaviour. This research was prompted by the ageing of the labour force and the decline in labour force participation in the Netherlands in the past few decades. Research is focused primarily on the importance of financial incentives (wage rates, social security benefits, and (early) retirement benefits), health, job characteristics and social environment as determinants of retirement behaviour.

The baseline survey for the CERRA dataset was conducted in 1993, with the first follow-up in 1995. Waves 3 and beyond are planned for later years, although currently no funding is available to finance these waves. The first wave of the CERRA panel contains information on 4,727 Dutch households in which the head of the household was aged between 43 and 63 in 1993 (3,581 aged 53-63 and 1,145 aged 43-52). Both the head of household and their spouse were interviewed. The questionnaire consists of several sections: a household section covering, amongst other things, age, sex, nationality, family composition, and education; a labour market section covering job characteristics, earnings, benefit levels, job search behaviour, early retirement schemes, job mobility within the firm, expectations and future plans, and job history; a health section with self-evaluations of health, epidemiology, health care, health use/consumption, health insurance; a housing and housing mobility section; and a financial situation section covering wealth and outstanding debts. In structure and contents, the CERRA panel was designed to be comparable to the Health and Retirement Survey (HRS) conducted by the University of Michigan Survey Research Centre in the U.S. The effect of work environment and availability of retirement options are being studied through an additional survey of Dutch firms. An organisational survey of approximately 750 companies where respondents currently or previously worked was undertaken in 1994 to supplement the household survey. The first wave of data will be made available in 1996 for academic researchers through the Steinmetz Archives in Amsterdam.

7.2.2 OPCS RETIREMENT SURVEYS
Rebecca J Goldman, Principal Investigator
Institute for Fiscal Studies, London, United Kingdom
Dates: 1996 - 1996

The goal of the project is to understand how circumstances change at the time of and shortly after retirement, and factors influencing these changing circumstances. This study analyses the two-wave `Retirement Survey cohort' which was conducted by the Office of Population Censuses and Surveys (OPCS). The first wave, in 1988/9, was of a nationally-representative sample of about 3,500 people aged between 55 and 69 years in private households and their partners, with data collection by personal interview. Five years later, in 1994, the surviving sample and their current partners were re-interviewed to obtain longitudinal information about their transition to and through retirement. The 1994 survey was conducted by Computer Assisted Personal Interviewing (CAPI). Interviews were completed with about 2,250 respondents aged 70-74 years and an additional 310 partners outside this age-group. Topics covered include income, assets, housing, pension entitlements, disability, caring responsibilities, retirement, and labour market participation.

7.2.3 THE LUXEMBOURG INCOME STUDY & LUXEMBOURG EMPLOYMENT STUDY
Timothy Smeeding, Project Director
Luxembourg Income Study, Luxembourg, and Syracuse University, Syracuse, NY, USA
Dates: 1983 - Ongoing

The purpose of the LIS project is to collect in one location household microdata on incomes and economic status of families of all ages for a large number of developed and transitional countries for use in cross-national analysis of social policy issues related to income distribution. Since its inception in 1983, the experiment has grown into a cooperative research project with a membership that includes countries in Europe, North America, the Far East and Australia. The database now contains a total of over 60 datasets from more than 25 countries covering the period 1968 to 1992. During 1996, additional surveys will be added to more fully represent the period of the middle 1990s for most of the nations. Negotiations are underway to add data from additional countries, including Korea, Mexico, Portugal and South Africa.

Research using these data has examined such topics as: international comparisons of income distributions and poverty; gender wage and poverty differentials; the effects of economic transitions in Central and Eastern Europe on poverty and income inequality; and poverty of the elderly and of children in families.

The Luxembourg Employment Study (LES) has recently been added to the LIS project. The aim of the LES is to provide internationally comparable micro data in the field of labour market research on job search, employment characteristics, comparable occupations, etc. LES makes available to researchers a set of labour force surveys from the early 1990's from countries with quite different market structures (member states of the European Union, other Western European countries (EFTA), Central and Eastern European transition countries, and overseas countries). The LES team has harmonised and standardised the microdata from the labour force surveys in order to facilitate comparative research.

Findings from both studies have been published in a number of books and research journals, as well as in over 150 LIS-LES working papers. A list of these working papers may be found on the LIS web site at the URL http://lissy.ceps.lu/wpapers.htm (http://www-cpr. maxwell.syr.edu/lis_part/lispaps.htm in the United States).

7.2.4 DUTCH SOCIO-ECONOMIC PANEL STUDY (DSEP)
Arie Kapteyn, Principal Investigator
Economics Institute Tilburg (EIT), Tilburg, The Netherlands
Dates: 1985-1991

The Dutch Socio-Economic Panel Study (DSEP) is as nationally representative panel of individuals and households modelled after the U.S. Panel Study of Income Dynamics (PSID). Each wave of the panel data set consists of about 5,000 households. The data set contains information about the following variables: Net income, plus a breakdown into income components, (e.g. earnings, interest income); level and composition of asset holdings of households; ownership of durable consumption goods; demographic characteristics of the household; labour force participation, (desired) number of hours of work; poverty status of the household and economic position of the household.

Findings from this study were presented in:

> Muffels, R. J. A. 1995. "The dynamics of income and deprivation of the elderly", presented at the III European Congress of Gerontology, Amsterdam, 30 August - 2 September 1995.

7.2.5 THE VSB SAVINGS PROJECT
Arie Kapteyn, and Ellen Katrine Nyhus, Principal Investigators
Economics Institute Tilburg (EIT), Tilburg, The Netherlands
Dates: 1993 - ongoing

The goal of the project is to contribute to a better understanding of household savings and household financial decision-making. The project makes use of two sources of data. The first is a panel of Dutch households (DSEP), described elsewhere in this report. The second is the VSB-panel. This is a panel of 3,000 households, begun in 1993, of which 2,000 form a representative sample of the Dutch population and 1,000 households are drawn from the top 10 percent of the income distribution. All participating households have a personal computer at home and the questionnaires are completely computerised. The contents of the questionnaire is rather similar to that of the DSEP panel, but more emphasis is laid on the measurement of assets, consumption also is measured and a set of psychological questions have been added, including questions about their attitudes towards risk, time preference, expectations, financial planning, bequest motives, personality traits, life expectancy, etc. The first wave of the VSB-panel became available in April 1994. The data cover all ages, but a representative sample of those aged 55 and over is available and the oversample of the top 10 percent of the income distribution contains an over-representation of older households.

Findings from this study have been published in a series of reports from the VSB Project published by the Economics Institute Tilburg (EIT). A description of the project, a listing of progress reports and copies of the questionnaire may be obtained at the following World Wide Web site: http://cwis.kub.nl/~few5/center/research/vsb.htm.

7.2.6 SAVINGS AND PENSIONS: STRUCTURAL ANALYSIS OF HOUSEHOLD SAVINGS AND WEALTH POSITIONS OVER THE LIFE CYCLE
Arie Kapteyn, Principal Investigator
Economics Institute Tilburg (EIT), Tilburg, The Netherlands
Dates: 1995 - ongoing

The overall objective of the research is to improve the understanding of financial decision-making by individuals and households, particularly with respect to savings, investment (portfolio choice), and financial provision for old age. On the basis of micro-datasets from different countries, both fundamental and applied research into household and individual financial decision making will be undertaken. Furthermore, laboratory experiments will be part of the project and economists, econometricians and psychologists will collaborate. The fundamental research topics studied include the precautionary, bequest and other motives for saving; and experimental work on time preference, risk aversion, and decision-making about savings. Applied work will include the relation between private savings and pension provisions; portfolio choice, diversification and taxes; saving behaviour and wealth position of the elderly; asset accumulation, early retirement schemes and labour supply; labour supply, liquidity constraints, savings and housing demand.

This project will use three types of empirical data: (1) The VSB-panel (described elsewhere in this report) will be made available to all teams; (2) Survey data concerning household finances for the United Kingdom, Italy, United States, The Netherlands, Germany, and Sweden will be used by the separate teams to perform analyses that pertain to the country concerned, and also in comparative studies across countries; (3) Laboratory experiments conducted at Tilburg will provide the third source of empirical data.

7.2.7 THE GERMAN SOCIO-ECONOMIC PANEL (GSOEP) AND ENGLISH LANGUAGE PUBLIC USE FILES
Gert G. Wagner, and Richard Burkhauser, Principal Investigators
Deutsches Institut für Wirtschaftsforschung (DIW), Berlin Germany, and Syracuse University, Syracuse, NY, USA
Dates: 1984-Ongoing.

The German Socio-Economic Panel (GSOEP) allows researchers to follow the demographic, sociological and economic outcomes of a random sample of the population of re-united Germany. Because the data on people living in the western states of Germany began in 1984, it is possible to follow these households for six years before re-unification and for all years following reunification. Detailed information on income, housing, and living arrangements allow researchers to look at economic well-being, satisfaction, health, and care-giving relationships, both cross-sectionally and longitudinally. Detailed questions on work history and education allow the consequences of work on economic well-being at older ages and to look at retirement behaviour to be traced.

The design for the GSOEP is based on the design of the American Panel Study of Income Dynamics (PSID). A representative sample of people living in private households in the western States of Germany have been followed since 1984. The sample includes an oversample of guest workers. To account for the reunification of Germany and for new immigrants who have moved to the western States of Germany since 1984, these two additional samples have been made available. The data contain a core set of questions on income, housing, household characteristics, and living arrangements that are asked each year. Modules on specific topics (health, retirement, family history, etc.) have been included each year.

The survey was not intended to specialize on the older population, but 3,440 persons in the 1990 reunited Germany sample were aged 55 and over in 1992. In addition, over the next decade, 2,231 more respondents will move into that age range. The data allow either cross-sectional analysis on a representative sample of Germans or temporal analyses of a representative sample of Germans over time. The English language file provides a method for the GSOEP data to be accessed by scholars living outside of Germany. The initial wave of the public use file of the GSOEP in 1984 is a random 95 percent sample of the original data with 11,610 respondents in 5,624 households and contains most of the original variables. These data also have been linked by Syracuse University to the U.S. PSID for comparative analyses. The data file currently contains data from 1983 to 1990 on over 25,000 Americans and 17,000 Germans.

Information about the linked data and copies of the codebooks may be obtained in English from the World Wide Web Site: http://www-cpr.maxwell.syr.edu/gsoep/equivfil.htm. Information on the original Sozio-oekonomische Panel can be found at http://www.diw-berlin.de/soep/ (in German and in English).

7.2.8   INTERNATIONAL RETIREMENT MIGRATION OF BRITONS TO SOUTHERN EUROPE

Anthony Warnes, Russell King, and Allan Williams, Principal Investigators
University of Sheffield, Sheffield, United Kingdom.
Dates: 1994 - 1997

This project is investigating patterns of international retirement migration in Europe The goals of the study are to: develop improved current estimates and historical time-series of the number of retired persons from the United Kingdom and European Union who are temporarily and permanently living in southern Europe; and describe the social, demographic and economic characteristics of these migrants and the decision process by which they select their destinations. The investigators intend to generate data that can used in projections of future migration flows within Europe.

Time series estimates of international migration flows will be derived through secondary analysis of existing information from Eurostat and other sources. Both quantitative and qualitative surveys are being conducted in 1995 and 1996 of British citizens aged 50 or older who reside more than six months of each year in Southern Europe (Portugal, Spain, Italy, Cyprus and Malta). Information collected in the surveys includes data on work histories, expectations for retirement, retrospective accounts of financial family and health information, post-migration events, and satisfaction with destination. Comparative surveys of return migrants in the United Kingdom also are being conducted.

7.2.9 LIFE COURSE OF 2 COHORTS OF RETIREES: GREATER PARIS REGION

Françoise Cribier, Principal Investigator
Équipe de Géographie Sociale et Gérontologie
CNRS-University Paris 7, Paris, France
Dates: 1972 - 2000

The main goal of this project was to reconstruct retrospectively the main features of the life course of two cohorts of Parisians, 12 years apart, from birth to retirement and to observe this population prospectively forward from retirement. The data collected are used to analyse work, family and residential histories of the elderly and ways of life since retirement, according to social class and characteristics.

This longitudinal study of the life-course of two cohorts of Parisians, those first drawing their pension in 1972 (born 1907-12) and in 1984 (born 1919-24) uses several sources of data: National Pension Fund (CNAVTS) records on working life, retirement, pension, marital status, children, place of residence, etc.; vital statistics; and surveys. The surveys conducted by this research group address broad social, economic and demographic questions, as well as interviews of sub-samples on such topics as residential mobility in the Paris area or to the provinces, patterns of holiday-making and double residence, co-residence with children or siblings, ageing in place, etc., as well as life histories. The survey panel represents a sample of 1:80 of the 110,000 newly retired of 1972 (n=1,370), and a sample of 1:160 of the 130,000 newly retired of 1984 (n=800). The two samples are stratified to be representative of the retired Parisians salaried of the private sector. Findings from this study were reported in:

Cribier, Françoise. 1995. "Attitudes to retirement and to family relationships in two cohorts of retired Parisians", presented at the III European Congress of Gerontology, Amsterdam, 30 August - 2 September 1995.

7.2.10 WORK AND RETIREMENT AMONG OLDER WORKERS IN FINLAND: A THREE-YEAR FOLLOW-UP STUDY
P. Huuhtanen and M. Piispa, Principal Investigators
Finnish Institute of Occupational Health, Helsinki, Finland

As a part of the Finn-Age research programme, interviews were carried out dealing with attitudes toward work and retirement. The study sample consisted of 1,395 persons over 35 years of age in the Finnish labour force (51% women). The second sample comprised 388 persons between the ages of 35 and 64 years who were receiving pension income. Data were collected by telephone interviews in connection with the Labour Force Survey compiled by Statistics Finland in 1994.

Among the topics addressed in the interviews were the prevalence of serious thought being given to the possibility of early retirement, and the importance of health and functional ability, occupation, sector of employment, job security, pace and improvements in work environment, time schedule and content for predicting retirement expectations. Comparisons were conducted of workers in municipal and private sectors, and with pensioners. Findings were reported in:

Huuhtanen, P. and M. Piispa. 1995. "Factors associated with thoughts of early retirement" and "Health and work capacity as reasons for early retirement in the Finnish private and public sector: A three-year follow-up study", presented at the III European Congress of Gerontology, Amsterdam, 30 August - 2 September 1995.

7.2.11 POPULATION AGEING AND INTER-GENERATIONAL EQUITY IN PENSION SYSTEMS
Christopher Prinz, Principal Investigator
European Centre for Social Welfare Policy and Research
Vienna, Austria
Dates: 1995 - 1997

The aim of this project is to compare the existing generational contracts in terms of pensions in four European countries: Austria, Germany, Sweden and the United Kingdom. For each country, total pension contributions and benefits paid/received by all cohorts born in the 20th century are being estimated and analysed. Demographic and pension models for the period 1920 to 2080 are being developed. Preliminary findings are described in:

Gonnot, Jean-Pierre, Nico Keilman and Christopher Prinz. 1996. *Social Security, Household, and Family Dynamics in Ageing Societies*, European Studies of Population, The Hague: Netherlands Interdisciplinary Demographic Institute.

7.2.12 TRANSITIONS TO RETIREMENT
Hans-Dieter Schneider, Principal Investigator
University of Fribourg, Fribourg, Switzerland
Dates: 1993 - 1997

This project aims to describe the transition to retirement through a life span developmental approach.   Particular attention is paid to the combination of societal and individual level resources used in successful adaptation to retirement. Retirement transitions are analysed for a total sample of 680 German-speaking Swiss retirees. Both a structured longitudinal survey and a qualitative diary study were conducted. For the entire sample, information was collected on psychological well-being and personality characteristics, adaptation to retirement, social networks of respondents, job characteristics and leisure activities, and current economic status and living conditions, as well as use of pre-retirement planning. These standardised instruments were administered three times: 6 months prior to retirement and again 6 and 18 months after retirement. Additional analyses are being conducted to compare those respondents who retired early (n=177) with those who retired on-time for differences in both determinants and outcomes. For 203 respondents, additional interviews were conducted with the spouses/partners in order to assess the effects of retirement on the marriage/partnership. In an additional sample, (13 respondents in Switzerland and 13 in Germany) open-ended, semi-structured diaries were used to obtain in-depth information.

7.3 SOCIAL ASPECTS

7.3.1 LIVING ARRANGEMENTS AND SOCIAL NETWORKS OF OLDER ADULTS (NESTOR-LSN)
Cees P.M. Knipscheer, Jenny De Jong Gierveld, T.G. van Tilburg and Pearl Dykstra, Principal Investigators
Vrije Universiteit Amsterdam, Amsterdam, The Netherlands
Dates: 1990 - 1995

The purposes of the NESTOR research project entitled 'Living Arrangements and Social Networks of Older Adults (LSN)' were to provide insight into the determinants and outcomes of living arrangements of older adults, and to construct models to predict future trends. The perspective taken in this study emphasises the autonomy of older adults, focusing on the effect of social networks on an older person's capacity for independent living. Measures of well-being include support received, daily functioning, and coping with life events. A survey of 4,494 adults aged 55 to 89 years in the Netherlands was undertaken in 1992 to collect information on living arrangements, health, and social network composition. A 1993 follow-up study of transitions in support networks for respondents born between 1908 and 1937 was conducted through the Longitudinal Ageing Study of Amsterdam (LASA) which will monitor the respondents up to the year 2000 in three waves. In addition, part of the questionnaire is being replicated with a sample of older adults in Tuscany, Italy. Cross-national comparisons will be made with respect to the network characteristics of the elderly in both countries. Results are summarized in English in:

> Knipscheer, Cees P. M., J. de Jong Gierveld, T.G. van Tilburg and Pearl A. Dykstra. 1995. *Living Arrangements and Social Networks of Older Adults*, Amsterdam: VU University Press.

7.3.2 GERMAN AGEING SURVEY
Martin Kohli and Freya Dittmann-Kohli, Principal Investigators
Freie Universität Berlin, Germany, and University of Nijmegen,
Nijmegen, The Netherlands
Dates: 1994 - 1997

The German Ageing Survey is an interdisciplinary project that examines sociological and psychological questions of adulthood and ageing. Objective life conditions and subjective self- and life-conceptualizations of the current and future cohorts of the German elderly are assessed. A survey of 5,000 German persons aged 40-85 years old will be conducted. The sociological component (designed by the Research Group on Ageing and the Life Course, Freie Universität Berlin) focuses on objective life conditions in six life domains: family and social networks; paid and unpaid work; social and political participation and leisure activities; health, housing, financial conditions; and intergenerational relations and transfers.

The psychological component of the German Ageing Survey comprises four dimensions of self and life conceptualizations: (1) standardized psychological indicators of well-being and life satisfaction; (2) evaluations of present, past and future life conditions and desired change in eight life domains; (3) conceptualizations of the ageing process in the domains of physical, psychological, social, and time use; and (4) measures of self-knowledge and its influence on life management and interpretations of experiences.

7.3.3 BANGOR LONGITUDINAL STUDY OF AGEING
G. Clare Wenger, Principal Investigator
Centre for Social Policy Research and Development, University of Wales
Bangor, United Kingdom
Dates: 1978 - ongoing

The main objective of this study is to describe the support networks of older people and measure changes in these networks both longitudinally and cross-sectionally. One of the major outcomes of the study has been the development of a support network typology, operationalised for use by clinicians and in further research. The study also examines a wide range of social variables including demographic characteristics, migration history, housing and financial circumstances, social contacts, sources of informal care, use of domiciliary services, and access to and use of formal health services. Major research questions investigated include whether rural and urban elderly have the same informal support and level of access to services, if networks are related to outcome measures (e.g., subjective health status, service use, and survival), and to understand how networks change and adapt over time.

The study was originally designed to look at access to various services and the availability of formal and informal support. After the first survey in 1979 it developed into a longitudinal study with survivors traced and followed up at four-year intervals (1983, 1987, 1991, 1995). A further wave will be conducted in 1999. The original sample was 534 people aged 65 and over living in their own homes in a cross-section of communities in Wales, weighted to ensure representativeness on the basis of marital status and gender. Subsequent interviews followed-up those who had entered long-stay institutional care. In addition to quantitative data, interviewers were asked to record verbatim other relevant qualitative data. From 1983- 1987 an intensive study of 30 people was conducted during which respondents were visited two to four times a year. The 1995 survey of survivors (n=95) concentrated specifically on measures of successful ageing, substitutability in sources of informal help, childlessness and friendship processes in later life, post-retirement moves, income and pensions, and a comparison of outcomes before and after community care reforms. One-third of these respondents were randomly recruited into a second intensive study sample and will be interviewed 2-3 times in the 18 months following the survey interview.

The results from this project have been published in a large number of research journals. Some of the articles include:

Wenger, G. Clare. 1990. "Change and Adaptation in Informal Support Networks of Elderly People in Wales 1979-1987". *Journal of Aging Studies*, 4(4):375-389

Wenger, G. Clare. 1995. "A Comparison of Urban and Rural Support Networks: Liverpool and North Wales". *Ageing and Society*, 15:59-81

General information about the study also may be obtained at the World Wide Web site: http://www.bangor.ac.uk/csprd/longitud.htm.

7.3.4 RELATIONS BETWEEN GENERATIONS AND FAMILY SUPPORT TO ELDERLY PEOPLE
Ms. Claudine Attias-Donfut, Principal Investigator
Caisse Nationale d'Assurance Vieillesse, Paris, France.
Dates: 1992 - ongoing

The main aim of this project is to study relations within multigenerational families, how family members cope with the costs and benefits of family support, and how formal care is used in relation to informal family help. Relations among three successive adult generations were studied with regard to issues touching upon health, leisure, daily life, relationships, services, financial transfers, and inheritance. This project specifically deals with the support given to older family members and to young adults entering the labour market.

The goal was to obtain a sample of multigenerational families representative in dimensions of familial solidarity, social solidarity, and geographical proximity, totalling about 5,000 people in 2,000 three-generation families. A sample in the "pivot generation" (G2) was first identified, and formed the basis on which the two other generations (G1 and G3) were obtained. Representatives of each of three generations were interviewed in 995 cases, but for 963 families only two generations could be interviewed. Project results have been published in French in:

> Attias-Donfut, Claudine (ed.).1995. Les Solidarités entre générations: Vieillesse, Familles, État, Paris: Nathan Série « Sciences Sociales ».

7.3.5 THE VULNERABLE ELDERLY AND ELDER POLITICS
Eigil Hansen
AKF, Institute of Local Government Studies, Copenhagen, Denmark
Dates: 1994 - 1995

The focus of this project was to evaluate the living condition of the vulnerable elderly living in the community in Denmark. In particular, the project sought to identify insufficiencies in housing and long-term care experienced by older persons, and to understand the preferences that they may have for security, welfare and need fulfilment. The project also examined the effect that different policies on care of the elderly have on their need for accommodation and assistance, and how housing and other services offered to the elderly vary according to the different types of local authorities. The survey included a systematic investigation of differences between urban and rural local authorities and between eastern and western Denmark.

The study was carried out in 75 of the 275 Danish municipalities, stratified into three types of local authorities offering high, intermediate, and low ratios of housing and nursing home services to the population age 70 and over. In all, 1,845 people aged 80 and over (662, 657 and 526 people in high, low and intermediate coverage authorities, respectively) were interviewed. In addition, telephone interviews were carried out in 6 sample areas with 75 persons indicated by the elderly themselves as close relatives or friends and with employees of the local social and health administration concerning the authorities' policy on the elderly. The survey of services offered to the elderly by various local authorities was based on a questionnaire sent to all Danish local authorities at the beginning of 1995.

7.3.6 TEENAGERS REACH RETIREMENT AGE: A LONGITUDINAL STUDY.
Sol Seim, Principal Investigator
Norwegian Institute of Gerontology, Oslo, Norway
Dates: 1939 - April 1996

This project characterises the psychological development of personality and intelligence over the life course through qualitative interviews, and psychological testing in a long-term prospective longitudinal study. The project leader followed a small group of persons from when they were 13 years old in 1939, contacting them when they were in their 30's and 60's and finally in 1994 when the participants were about 70 years old. The total duration of the project covers a period of more than 50 years. The data from the fourth follow-up is currently being processed for the 49 survivors of the 80 children in the original sample. Findings from the study covering the first three waves are reported in:

Seim, Sol. 1989. Teenagers Become Adult and Elderly: Intelligence and Personality from 13 to 30 to 60 years. Oslo: Norwegian Institute of Gerontology, Report 5.

7.3.7 WOMEN AS THEY AGE: A CHALLENGE
Gilbert Dooghe and Lieve Vanderleyden, Principal Investigators
CBGS, Ministry Flemish Community, Brussels, Belgium
Dates: 1992 - 1993

This project was a comprehensive study of the social and economic well-being of women 55 years and older in Belgium, making use of data on the older population in Belgium collected previously in 1979 and 1985. The main purpose of the study was to examine older women as a potentially vulnerable group within the older population and to assess whether the situation of older women had worsened over the time between the two surveys. Special attention was given to the physical and psychological health of elderly women, including functioning, medical conditions, subjective health evaluation, functioning, and use of health care services, as well as questions about sexuality, self-image, and depression. The project also analysed gender differences in several aggregate demographic, social and economic components of ageing in Belgium, including the female advantage in life expectancy, sex differences in mortality and morbidity, employment rates, economic status, and household structure.

7.3.8 THE ELDERLY WOMEN IN EUROPE: CHOICES AND CHALLENGES.
Gilbert Dooghe, Principal Investigator
CBGS, Ministry Flemish Community, Brussels, Belgium.
Dates: 1994 - 1995

This report was an outgrowth of the Belgian project listed above. Existing data from several European countries were compiled in book form to compare and contrast the economic, social, psychological and physical well-being of women. The main purpose of the study was to focus on women's situation because women make up the majority of both the older population and of caregivers in all of the European nations, and because elderly women are generally more vulnerable than elderly men, being poorer, more likely to be widowed, to be institutionalised, and generally having lower living standards. The study examined existing quantitative data from Denmark, the United Kingdom, Spain, Italy, the Netherlands and Belgium. The report is available in English as:

Dooghe G. and N. Appleton (eds.), Elderly Women in Europe: Choices and Challenges, Leuven, Belge: Centrum voor Bevolkingsen Gezins-studiën.

7.3.9 DAILY LIFE AMONG THE OLD-OLD AND THE OLDEST-OLD: A NORDIC COMPARATIVE STUDY.
Lars Andersson, Principal Investigator
Stockholm Gerontology Research Center
Stockholm, Sweden
Dates: 1989 - 1993

The main focus of this project was to understand the quality of life of the oldest-old in physical, psychosocial and existential domains. Research questions included the extent of loneliness and its relationship to health, functional capacity, and social networks; sense of coherence and its relationship to factors such as health, functional capacity, and social network; and the presence of meaning in life and its relationship to factors such as health, functional capacity, social network, and self-esteem. Representative samples were drawn from population registers in a sampled municipality in Sweden, Finland, and Norway. One hundred persons in each of the age groups 75-79, 80-84, and 85+ were interviewed.

7.3.10 ADULT EDUCATION FOR THE ELDERLY IN SCANDINAVIA.
Jan-Erik Ruth, Principal Investigator
Kuntokallio Center for Gerontological Training and Research, Östersundom, Finland.
Dates: 1988 - 1995

The purpose of the study was to investigate education for the aged as a part of the life-long learning process and to study the motives, obstacles, and the scope of participation of the elderly in adult education in Scandinavia. In 1991, a postal survey was sent to a random sample of 1,000 non-institutionalised men and women aged 65-85 in each of four countries: Finland, Sweden, Norway, and Denmark. Information collected includes participation in formal, informal and nonformal educational activities, as well as leisure activities among retirees in four Nordic countries. The background variables cover the type of community; income; and education of the respondent and the education of his/her family; experiences in school and further education; and a subjective evaluation of health, memory and learning capacity. The remaining questions dealt with reasons for participation as well as obstacles to non-participation in adult education.

7.4 HEALTH CARE SERVICE USE

7.4.1 INFORMAL SUPPORT FOR THE ELDERLY (PART I AND II)
Manuel Justel, Principal Investigator
Centro de Investigaciones Sociológicas, Madrid, Spain
Dates: 1993 - 1995

The primary purpose of this project was to investigate the role played by the extended family in providing long-term care to older persons in the community. Previous research.in Spain was mainly devoted to the study of institutionalised elderly. Two surveys were conducted to obtain information on the health, living conditions and informal long-term care arrangements of community-dwelling older persons in Spain. The intention of the data collection was to assess the kind and sources of assistance needed and received by older persons, as well as to on the assistance they may be providing to their own families. In 1993, a national sample of 2,500 men and women, aged sixty five and over was interviewed regarding their health, living conditions and care needs and the extent and features of the care they receive. This was followed by a second survey of 1,702 informal caregivers to dependent elderly. This survey provided detailed information about types of help, and the frequency and timing of care. Special attention was paid to motivation and caregiver burden.

7.4.2 TRANSPORT FOR ELDERLY PERSONS: MOBILITY SURVEY OF TEN COUNTIES IN ENGLAND & WALES
Francis Jegede, Principal Investigator
University of Derby, Derby, United Kingdom
Dates: 1993 - 1998

The purpose of this project is to investigate the role of transport in the economic, social and psychological well-being of older people in Britain. Advancing age can effectively reduce access to and use of public transport. There is, as yet, no consensus on how best to address the problem. The first survey highlights the geographic variations in demand, provision and use of public transport across counties in England and Wales. The specific aims of these surveys are to: examine the experiences of elderly people in the use of public transport in England and Wales; conduct an inter-county analysis of mobility situations of elderly persons with a view toward regional variations in access to and use of public transport; prepare a database and first hand field experience upon which further research on services for elderly people could be built; identify the transport needs of elderly people according to their personal circumstances and the local conditions; and provide some recommendations that could inform transport operators and policy makers on the best way to improve elderly people's access to public transport.

This survey was conducted using self-administered postal questionnaires sent to 2,000 persons 60 years and older in ten counties of England and Wales. The questionnaire was designed to gain insight into the socio-economic, health and mobility conditions of elderly people in each of these counties. In particular, the access to and ability to use public transport was specifically addressed in the context of respondents' local and long distance movement needs. A random sample of 200 respondents in each county was drawn from the Family Health Services Authorities data base.

7.4.3 USE OF OPEN AND INSTITUTIONAL CARE POLICIES FOR THE DEPENDENT ELDERLY

Anja Noro, Principal Investigator
National Research and Development Centre for Welfare and Health, Helsinki, Finland
Dates: 1991 - 1995

The main purpose of this study was to evaluate the de-institutionalisation policy for elderly persons in Finland enacted between 1981 and 1991. This question was addressed through policy analysis using official data on de-institutionalisation rates among the population aged 65 years and over in long-term care, adjusted for the changes in total population at risk by age. Data also were collected on changes in the case-mix of patients in long-term care facilities by age and dependency level and in length of stay over the decade. The second goal of the study was to assess the appropriateness of institutional or home care and evaluate older patients' own experiences and preferences for care. Appropriateness of care as assessed by both patients and residential care personnel was evaluated in terms of patient characteristics. Comparisons also were conducted of health-related quality of life (HRQOL) and functional ability among non-institutionalised and institutionalised elderly.

The investigators are currently engaged in an analysis of the appropriateness of discharge plans for de-institutionalisation of the least dependent patients from residential care. The data used are from one-day censuses of institutionalised people in all public and private residential homes and health centre hospitals (or nursing homes) in Finland, which were carried out in 1981, 1986, and 1991; and a survey of moderately independent persons aged 65-84 in residential care conducted by the investigators in 1992.

7.4.4 ACCEPTANCE AND BENEFITS OF EXTENDED IN-HOME SERVICES FOR RURAL ELDERLY NEEDING CARE.

Hartmut Radebold, Principal Investigator
University of Kassel, Kassel, Germany
Dates: 1993 - 1996

The main purpose of the research project is to evaluate a new combination of in-home services in selected rural regions in Germany. The research was undertaken to reduce the number of individuals unnecessarily institutionalised by reducing the degree of helplessness through rehabilitation and optimizing in-home services so that they fit the individual requiring assistance. The project has sought to identify the necessary measures needed to achieve an optimal care supply network for elderly people.

Beginning in November 1993, existing services for in-home nursing care in two mainly rural regions were experimentally supplemented by counselling through social workers and rehabilitation measures performed by different kinds of therapists. Using these interventions as a basis for study, a portrait of the typical course of home care was compiled, including the role of different health care professions, use of aids, and the success of different types of interventions in terms of rehabilitation. Included in the research were analyses of predictors of service utilisation including age, level and types of disability, living arrangements, and psychiatric problems. Information also was solicited on how the target population obtained knowledge of the existence of the new services, and needs specific to the rural elderly.

7.5 MULTI- AND INTER-DISCIPLINARY

7.5.1 BERLIN AGING STUDY (DIE BERLINER ALTERSSTUDIE) (BASE)
Paul Baltes, Principal Investigator
Max Planck Institute for Human Development and Education, Berlin, Germany
Dates: 1989 - 1997

The primary objective of the Berlin Ageing Study (BASE) is to make a broad-based, in-depth, multi- and interdisciplinary longitudinal assessment and analysis of ageing, involving internal medicine and geriatrics, psychiatry, psychology, sociology, economics and social policy. The study is designed to address three principal questions: (1) the prediction of age differences from life-history data; (2) the degree and direction of variation within the domains identified by each discipline; and (3) interdisciplinary relationships between age differences and defined levels of functioning. The longitudinal continuation of the study aims to complete the picture of age differences obtained with cross-sectional data to enable: (1) recording of ageing processes; (2) assessment of temporal stability of individual life courses; and (3) testing of causal hypotheses on determinants of ageing. Examples of areas of interest are questions of selective longevity and mortality in old age, the early (pre-pathological) and differential diagnosis of dementia, the development of the need for care (its dimensions and specific forms), and the phenomenon of terminal decline before death.

Information collected on the study population includes: Social - life course antecedents and generational experiences, later phases of the family life course, social resources and social participation, economic conditions and the provision of care. Psychological - intelligence and cognition, self and personality, social functioning and social networks, current correlates of psychiatric morbidity and co-morbidity, neuropsychological functioning and coping with psychiatric morbidity. There is also a special investigation of the "subdiagnostic morbidity" of psychic disturbances. Medical objective and subjective health, functional capacity, risk profiles, multimorbidity and medical treatment.

BASE started as a cross-sectional study, but has been expanded into a cohort-sequential longitudinal study. Data collection for the baseline cross-sectional study took place from May 1990 until June 1993. It used a representative and heterogeneous sample from west Berlin, with an age range between 70 and 105 years, stratified by age and sex, thus oversampling the very old and men. The study allowed three levels of participation differentiated by the amount of contact and intensity of assessment, ranging from: (1) a short initial contact (n = 1,219); (2) completion of a multidisciplinary intake assessment (n=928); and (3) participation in the study's intensive protocol involving on average 14 sessions (n = 516). Methods ranged from biochemical analyses through psychological tests to interviews and social survey methodologies. The longitudinal study started with a second comprehensive follow-up assessment using a revised version of the cross-sectional intake assessment (June 1993 to May 1994). Participants were survivors of the main study's key sample (n = 377). A second six-session follow-up (n = 324) was conducted between March 1995 and August 1996. Results from the research are included in:

"Special Issue: The Berlin Aging Study". 1993. *Ageing and Society*, Vol. 13(4):475-680.

"Review Symposium: The Berlin Aging Study". 1994. *Ageing and Society*, 14: 589-617.

Mayer, K. U. and P. B. Baltes (Hg.). 1996. *Die Berliner Altersstudie*, Berlin: Akademie Verlag.

7.5.2 GERMAN INTERDISCIPLINARY LONGITUDINAL STUDY ON ADULTHOOD AND AGEING (ILSE)
Ursula Lehr, Principal Investigator
University of Heidelberg
Heidelberg, Germany
Dates: 1993 - Ongoing

The German Interdisciplinary Study on Adulthood and Ageing (ILSE) aims at investigating individual, historical, social and material conditions for healthy, self-determined and satisfied ageing. Because ageing is a multidimensional process, it is influenced not only by historical, social, economic, environmental and biological factors, but also by the interaction of the ageing person and his environment. ILSE is organised as a longitudinal study with a comparison of two birth-cohorts (1930-32 and 1950-52). Each of these age groups was influenced by different conditions before and after World War II in west and east Germany. ILSE also studies the influence of different social and economic conditions on life-expectancy, quality of life and health within cohorts through a multicentric study design within Germany.

The sample consists of 1,384 people in two cohorts: 1930-32 and 1950-52. The baseline data collection was conducted from May 1993 until April 1996. Participants are given a two-day examination covering such areas as: social and cognitive competence; life-management; personality attributes; attitudes; coping styles; well-being and life satisfaction; biographical data; biomedical variables including health-related behaviour physical activities, mental and physical health status; and biomedical indicators. There are six subsequent measurement points planned for every third year.

7.5.3 THE AUTONOMY OF THE AGEING POPULATION IN SWITZERLAND
Christian J. Lalive d'Epinay, Principal Investigator
Centre for Interdisciplinary Gerontology (CIG), Univ. of Geneva, Geneva, Switzerland
Dates: 1993 - 1997

The primary goal of this project is to establish a general overview of the living conditions of elderly Swiss people and examine change in these conditions over time. A second aim is to design and validate a life course position indicator (LCPI) based on three factors: functional health; family time-path position; and professional time-path position. The study combines cross-sectional survey research with a prospective longitudinal study and a retrospective comparison. A sample of 2,095 individuals representing the Swiss population aged 60 years old and over in an urban area (Geneva) and a semi-urban region (Central Valais) was collected in 1994. The initial sample was randomly selected from population registers and stratified by age, gender and region. The survey covers the following topics: medical conditions and symptomatology, functional limitation, depression, utilisation of health services, home and institutional care, social integration, participation, isolation; family and social networks and intergenerational relations. The longitudinal study of the 80-84 age group will focus on the factors related to preservation of the autonomy of elderly people, as well as identifying the factors which lead to institutionalisation. The 1994 findings will be compared to a similar study conducted 15 years ago in the same regions to identify the changes observed between an urban and semi-urban region over time.

7.6 OTHER PROJECTS

7.6.1 THE STATUS OF OLDER PERSONS IN ECE COUNTRIES: ECONOMIC CONDITIONS, LIVING ARRANGEMENTS, AND GENDER; and THE DYNAMICS OF POPULATION AGEING IN ECE COUNTRIES
Miroslav Macura, Chief; Nikolai Botev, Project Manager
Population Activities Unit, UN/ECE, Geneva, Switzerland
Dates: 1996 - Ongoing, 1992 - 1996

As part of two successive projects, the Population Activities Unit (PAU) of the United Nations Economic Commission for Europe (UN/ECE), has assembled a set of cross-nationally comparable micro-data samples based on the 1990-round national population and housing censuses. These data is being used to study the social and economic conditions of the elderly in selected countries in the ECE region.

The PAU's recommendations regarding the sample design and size envisaged: (1) drawing individual-based samples of about one million persons; (2) progressive oversampling with age in order to ensure sufficient presentation of various categories of older people; (3) retaining information on all persons co-residing in the sampled individual's dwelling unit. Most countries have drawn their samples in accordance with these principles. Some countries (specifically Estonia, Finland, Latvia and Lithuania) adhered to earlier PAU recommendations and included in their samples only the population over age 50 and the persons residing with them (Estonia, Latvia and Lithuania have provided the entire population over age 50, while Finland has sampled it with progressive over-sampling). Several countries provided samples that were not specifically drawn for this project, and cover the entire population without any oversampling.

The PAU was involved both in the drawing of the samples, and performs their processing. This includes cleaning (where necessary) and standardisation. Based on a study of census data comparability in the ECE region, a set of nomenclatures and classifications were adopted as standards for recoding. The data processing has been completed, or is under way, for 13 countries that have already submitted their samples. One more (the United Kingdom) has confirmed its participation in the project. Several other countries (Belgium, Italy, Poland) have expressed interest in the project, and negotiations on the terms of their participation have taken place at various points of time. Nine of the participating countries have agreed to have their samples archived at the ICPSR data archive. Various forms of clearances are necessary for the rest of the data sets, but provisions have been made to facilitate access to them by researchers.

7.6.1 BRITISH HOUSEHOLD PANEL STUDY (BHPS)
Jay Gershuny, Director
ESRC Research Centre on Micro-Social Change, Essex, United Kingdom
Dates: 1991 - Ongoing

The BHPS is a nationally representative panel study of households and individuals living in the United Kingdom. The design of the BHPS is similar in structure to the American PSID and the German GSOEP. Information collected includes household income, tenure and consumption, housing quality, socio-economic and demographic descriptions of individuals and neighbourhoods, residential mobility, health and health-care use, current employment and earnings, and socio-economic and political attitudes.

The panel comprises 5,552 households containing 20,736 adults aged 16 and older first interviewed in 1991 and annually thereafter. Three waves of the data (1991-1994) are now available. The fieldwork for waves 4 and 5 have been completed, and a computer assisted version of the BHPS is expected to go into the field in 1996. The majority of participants in the BHPS are young and middle aged adults, however, 2,916 persons in the sample were aged 55 and older as of the second wave (1992).

Research using these data has concentrated on trajectories of household income and poverty over time, inequality, household structure and living arrangements, employment, and the household economy. Access to the data is through the ESRC Research Centre on Micro-Social Change at the University of Essex. The data are available to researchers who sign a contract with ESRC agreeing to respect data confidentiality rules.

7.6.3 THE RUSSIA LONGITUDINAL MONITORING SURVEY (RLMS)
Namvar Zohoori, Principal Investigator
Carolina Population Center, Chapel Hill, North Carolina, USA
Dates: 1992 - Ongoing

The Russia Longitudinal Monitoring Survey (RLMS) was designed to monitor a wide-ranging set of issues related to the social safety net and the impacts of reform on the Russian people and their communities. The survey covers a wide variety of topics, including income and employment; expenditures, assets, and housing; health status and health service use of children, women, and other family members; environmental health, family planning, and poverty; and the well-being of the elderly.

The RLMS is a multi-purpose, household-based longitudinal interview survey of a representative sample of the Russian population. This survey design provides for longitudinal monitoring of behaviour and events at the community, individual, and household levels allowing researchers systematically to link changes in government policies to changes in important health, demographic, and economic outcomes The project also includes collection of anthropometric data; detailed monitoring of individuals' health status and dietary intake; and collection of relevant community-level data, including region-specific price data and community infrastructure data. Recent publications from the RLMS include:

Mroz, T. and B. M. Popkin. 1995. Poverty and the Economic Transition in the Russian Federation. *Economic Development and Cultural Change*, 44:111-141.

Popkin, B. M., N. Zohoori and A. Baturin. 1996. The Nutritional Status of the Elderly in Russia, 1992 through 1994. *American Journal of Public Health*, 86(3):355-60.

Further information may be obtained from the World Wide Web site: http://www.cpc.unc. edu/projects/rlms/

7.6.4 SURVEY OF PEOPLE 70 YEARS OR OVER
Árpád Mészáros, Principal Investigator
Hungarian Central Statistical Office, Budapest, Hungary
Dates: 1990 - 1995

This project involved both analysis of secondary data from the 1990 Hungarian Census, as well as primary quantitative data collection through a five-per-thousand sample survey on the living conditions and health status of the elderly carried out in November 1990, in the frame of the Unified System of Household Surveys. This project is being extended by a survey of 50-69 year olds (see below).

7.6.5 SURVEY ON PERSONS AGED 50 OR OVER (BORN IN 1944 OR EARLIER)
Árpád Mészáros, Principal Investigator
Hungarian Central Statistical Office, Budapest, Hungary
Dates: 1994 - 1996

This study is an extension of the 1990 survey of the 70 and over population in Hungary conducted in 1990 by the same research group (see above). The primary objective is to study the health status and living conditions of the population aged 50-69 with those 70 or over. The goal was to understand the impact of social and economic changes in Hungary in recent years on the lives of older persons. The 1990 survey dealt with the living conditions and health status of the population 70 or over at the early period of social and economic changes in Hungary. The new survey repeated many of the same questions, thus allowing comparisons between data, as well as a study of the effects of these changes on the elderly over the intervening period.

The study also was extended to cover a broader age range, now including those aged 50-69 in 1994. In the early 1990s, unemployment re-appeared and has affected principally those at the beginning and the end of working ages. This younger age group is divided into two categories according to economic activity, in order to study occupational characteristics and problems of those aged 50-59 just before retirement, and those aged 60-69 who are either in the late stages of economic activity or in the early stage of retirement. Persons aged 70 years or over were asked a more extensive series of questions about health, and capacity for independent living. Many of these questions are comparable to those asked in 1990.

7.6.6 LIVING CONDITIONS SURVEY IN LATVIA
Inta Vasaraudze, Principal Investigator
Central Statistical Bureau of Latvia, Riga, Latvia
Dates: 1994 - 1996

This project is a broad survey of the living conditions and socio-economic status of the Latvian population. The survey was conducted in September 1994, and is presently being analysed. The intention is to extend the survey to a time series by administering the questionnaire again in 5 years. It is not clear whether this will be a panel design or repeated cross-section. Information collected in the study includes household composition, marital status, education, income and wealth, employment, work environment, housing, health, access to and use of health services, personal safety, and participation in organisations (political, humanitarian, religious, cultural).

8.   SUMMARY OF SURVEYED PROJECT INVESTIGATOR RECOMMENDATIONS

Each of the respondents in the second wave of the ageing survey was invited to give their opinions and assessments of the current state and future needs of ageing research in Europe. Investigators were asked to describe their own plans for ageing research over the next 5 to 7 years, and their views as to the focus that ageing research in Europe should take in the next ten years. The responses tended to fall into a consistent set of categories:

a) Productive ageing. The investigators frequently raised the question of what the elderly have to contribute as they are increasingly healthy, economically independent and actively integrated into society as a whole. Several respondents linked this question to the future of social benefits for the elderly and for those of working age and their children, and others to the rights of older persons to have equivalent access to the privileges of citizenship with those in younger age groups.

b) Inequality. The investigation of class, sex, and race based differentials in health, mortality, and psychological well-being was raised by several researchers as an important area of future concern. Several researchers also emphasized the importance of targeting vulnerable older persons, particularly those at risk of poverty, those with unmet long-term care needs, and those with reduced social support such as the oldest-old, childless, and widowed elderly.

c) Health promotion. Another set of suggestions was related to the goal of prevention of disease and understanding of the role of risk factors for later life morbidity, mortality and institutionalisation.

d) Health care. The delivery of health care services to older persons also was considered to be a topic of importance, with the issue of quality of care also mentioned by a number of investigators as deserving of more attention. The study of medical technology and ageing also was raised in this context.

e) Methodology. Many of the investigators focused their suggestions on methodological considerations, with suggestions of more longitudinal research and cohort-comparison studies at the top of their lists. Others mentioned the importance of collecting clinical information, such as bio-markers of ageing and performance measures to supplement social surveys, and the linkage both of individual data and vital statistics and administrative records, but also among secondary data to conduct macro-level analyses of time-series trends. The importance of combining qualitative and quantitative data also was mentioned.

f) Macro-level research. Few investigators made suggestions for more macro-level topics of study, but some did suggest cross-national studies of the welfare mix of benefits, labour force trends, and the impact of retirement on economic inequality.

9. CONCLUSIONS

9.1 General Findings

The majority of European data collection efforts identified by the survey that focused specifically on the older population were concerned with the "well-being" of the elderly, either in terms of health and survival; economic status and poverty; social integration and support; or psychological well-being.

Most of these studies, however, focus on a specific aspect of elderly well-being rather than collecting information on the nexus of health-work-family dynamics that need to be studied to understand the aging process and project future pension and health care costs.

a) The greatest number focus on health. However, these studies of health and mortality are concerned mainly with trajectories of disease and functional change, and collected limited amounts of social, economic, and demographic information. They also are largely local studies of non-representative samples. Therefore, although many excellent longitudinal studies are being undertaken in this area, they remain limited in geographic scope and substantive complexity, leaving them more useful to answer clinical questions than to address broader policy questions on health and health care financing.

b) Studies of economic status and of work and retirement constitute the second major focus of the studies, and one which is growing rapidly, but few specifically represent the older population. For example, the U.S. Panel Study of Income Dynamics has now been replicated in several countries, and the Luxembourg Income Study is providing standardized cross-national time series data for a large number of countries, but all of these sources are household surveys representing the entire adult population.

More recently, the CERRA study of Economic Aspects Of Aging in the Netherlands has set out to replicate the U.S. Health and Retirement Survey, providing for the first time nationally representative data on the health, labour market, and family situation of the near-to retirement age population in a European country. The OPCS retirement surveys in Britain are also investigating the retirement process and post-retirement situation of similarly aged cohorts, but do not contain the comprehensive information of the CERRA or of the HRS and AHEAD

c) Family life and Intergenerational Transfers. A third area of interest in European research on the elderly is in family relations. Although interest in the transformation of the family has led to several original studies of the family life of older persons, incorporating longitudinal designs and innovative interviewing strategies, these studies focus almost exclusively on aspects of social support and are generally conducted as in-depth studies of small, non-representative samples. They cannot therefore provide the data needed to understand the future of social protection for the older population as changes in state provided benefits in both the U.S. and Europe are implemented. It should be supplemented by further information about the economic consequences of family change, particularly in the areas of intergenerational transfers, where changing family structures have combined with cohort and period differences in economic resources.

d) Cross-National Studies. A major development in recent years has been the attempt to collect and standardize national data across European and North American countries. One good example is the work of the REVES (Réseau Expérance de Vie en Santé) International Network on Healthy Life Expectancy to compile an International Database with comparable measures of healthy or disability-free life expectancy. Such efforts will be extremely useful in developing an understanding of the dynamics of morbidity and mortality change intertemporally and internationally. This effort has been severely hampered, however, by lack of reliable, national-level data on functional ability at the older ages.

There also are similar efforts being undertaken in the social and economic fields as well. The work of the ECE project *Dynamics of Population Ageing* and The *Luxembourg Income and Employment Studies* to produce databases for comparative purposes which illustrate the ways in which standardization and harmonization of basic measures can be accomplished using already existing data. In the former, census data, and in the latter, household survey data. A singular feature of each effort is the availability of data for households, as well as information about individuals.

e) Longitudinal designs. There is a definite movement toward longitudinal perspective in the design of many of the data collection efforts identified in this survey. Fully 24 of the projects report the use of longitudinal designs. However, attention must be paid to the representativeness of these surveys cross-sectionally as well, or their usefulness will be extremely limited. An additional element to take into account in longitudinal studies of ageing is the effect of early life events on well-being at older ages. It is essential to investigate the ways in which gains in child survival accomplished in this century have affected health at adult and older ages. This life-course perspective is also important in understanding the long-term effects of social and economic resources on the health of the elderly, and on the resources that they will have available to them as they age.

9.2 Future Research Needs

It is a fair judgment, even in recent years, that much of the social and bio-medical data collection in aging in Europe has been descriptive rather than analytical. Still, it is clear from this Survey that gains have been made in developing nationally representative studies of economics of aging and the retirement process and in longitudinal studies of health. Unfortunately, the economic studies tend to provide nationally representative data at the cost of not adequately over-sampling the older population, and the research on health has exchanged in-depth clinical assessment for representativeness and comparability.

Another important step in future research is to complement the social and economic information in household surveys with the collection of clinical measures such as performance tests and bio-assays, and the linkage of individual survey data with information from vital statistics and administrative records.

Investigations of variations in the ageing process and well-being of subgroups of the population also should be stimulated. Differences in fertility, mortality, and migration mean that different racial and ethnic groups are ageing at varying rates. In addition, flows of working age populations, and the ageing of the labour force have increased racial and ethnic diversity of the older population. Yet, little research has been done to examine the consequences of population ageing in the context of such compositional changes. Such research should acknowledge the variability in racial and ethnic groups in their social, economic and physical experience of ageing, as well as the implications of different age structures of these subgroups.

Most importantly, no large scale studies have been undertaken that collect information on the *full array* of health, economic, and family characteristics that are essential to make cross-national comparisons with ongoing research in the United States. There is now one project (CERRA) that is designed to compare with the U.S. Health and Retirement Survey, but there were no projects comparable to either the U.S. Study of the Asset and Health Dynamics of the Oldest-Old (AHEAD) or to the U.S. National Long-Term Care Surveys. This is a major drawback that needs to be redressed through new data collection, and needs to be undertaken soon, so that cohort comparisons may be made and analyses conducted to rigorously examine changes over time as well as across countries. It would be most useful to embark upon a data integration project for national level health information. It should be feasible to prepare comparable datafiles from the nationally representative Health Interview Surveys that have been undertaken for many years in most of the countries of Europe and such an effort would complement what the Luxembourg Income and Employment Surveys have done with economic data and the PAU Census project for demographic statistics.

10. ADDITIONAL BIBLIOGRAPHICAL REFERENCES

Christensen, K. and J. Vaupel. 1996. "Determinants of Longevity: Genetic, Environmental and Medical Factors". *The Journal of Internal Medicine*, 240(6):333-341.

Council of Europe. 1996. *Recent Demographic Developments in Europe*. Belgium: Council of Europe Publishing.

DaVanzo, J. (ed.). 1996. *Russia's Demographic Crisis*. Santa Monica, CA: RAND Center for Russian and Eurasian Studies.

Hantrais, L. and M-T. Letablier. 1996. *Families and Family Policies in Europe*. London : Addison Wesley Longman, Ltd.

Jones, H. and J. Millar. 1996. *The Politics of the Family*. Aldershot: Avebury Publishing Ltd.

Kinsella, K. and Y. Gist. 1995. Older Workers, Retirement and Pensions: *A Comparative International Chartbook*. Washington, D.C.: U.S. Bureau of the Census.

Manton, K. and J. Vaupel. 1995. "Survival after the Age of 80 in the United States, Sweden, France, England, and Japan". *The New England Journal of Medicine*, 333(18):1232-1235.

Myers, G. C. 1994. "Population Growth and Age Structure: Implications and Policy Responses,". *European Population Conference Proceedings*, Vol. 1, New York and Geneva: United Nations.

Ostner, I. 1993. "Whose Solidarity with Whom? The case of Women in old age in the European Community". *Aspects of Ageing: A Celebration of the European Year of Older People and Solidarity between Generations*. Kaim-Caudle, P., J. Keithley and A. Mullender, eds.), London : Whiting & Birch. (pp. 25-41).

Ploug, N. 1994. "The Welfare State in Liquidation?", *Recent Trends in Cash Benefits in Europe* Niels Ploug and Jon Kvist (eds.). *Social Security in Europe Report 4*. Copenhagen: Danish National Institute of Social Research.

United Nations. 1996a. *Demographic Yearbook, 1994*. New York: United Nations.

United Nations. 1996b. *Population and Vital Statistics Report*, Statistical Papers, Series A, Vol. XLVIII, No. 3.

Wise, D. A. (ed.). 1996. *Advances In The Economics Of Aging*. National Bureau of Economic Research Project Report series. Chicago and London: University of Chicago Press.

APPENDICES

11.1. Survey instruments:
11.1.1 Wave I Questionnaire
11.1.2 Wave II Questionnaire
11.3. Research Projects by Country
11.4. Contact Addresses

11.1.1 Survey Questionnaire
Wave I

A Survey of Ageing Research Projects in Europe

Sponsors:

The Population Activities Unit
United Nations Economic Commission for Europe
and
The National Institute on Aging
United States National Institutes of Health

I. GENERAL DESCRIPTION OF THE RESEARCH PROJECT

1. What is the title of the research project?

#   #

2. Please enter the expected beginning and ending dates of the project.

(Please enter dates in the following format: 1 July 1993.)

Beginning   #   #
Ending   #   #

3. Please state briefly the main purpose of the research project.

(Maximum two sentences)

#   #

4. Please provide keywords that describe this project's substantive areas of investigation.

(Please list three to five keywords that describe the project's main research themes. For example, retirement, labor force participation, disability trends, intergenerational transfers, etc. These keywords will be used for database searches and other computerized sorting.)

#   #

5. Please provide a general abstract for this project.

(Maximum 400 words describing your project as you would like to see them published in a directory of research activities. Please include the study design. For example, specify whether the project mainly involves primary data collection, secondary analysis of existing information, evaluation of government programs or policies, or other activities. Where appropriate, indicate whether it is a cross-sectional survey, a longitudinal study, or an on-going research or monitoring effort. Please also describe the data being collected and/or analyzed. For example, quantitative data may be census or survey data, vital statistics or administrative records. Qualitative data may include participant observation, case studies or focus groups. Please also note the form in which data are being used. Are they aggregate summary data, micro data, coded interviews, historical records, etc? Also include the selection criteria of the units and, if appropriate, the sampling fraction).

#   #

IF YOUR PROJECT INVOLVES PRIMARY DATA COLLECTION THROUGH SURVEY RESEARCH, PLEASE ANSWER THE FOLLOWING QUESTIONS:

(Responses to the following four questions will be used to identify research projects, based on original data collection, that should be included in the second wave of this survey. These answers will not be included in the directory.)

6. Please describe the sample size or the number of people surveyed.

       #   #

7. What larger population does this sample represent?

       #   #

8. Of how many questions does your questionnaire consist?

       #   #

9. Could this questionnaire, or parts of it, be used in a cross-national survey of several European countries?

(Please answer with "Yes" or "No")

       #   #

II. PERSONAL INFORMATION
(Please provide complete information for only the principal investigator or project manager. Please enter Mr., Mrs., Miss, or Ms. for a person's title.)

MANAGER'S PERSONAL INFORMATION:

Title: #   #

Last Name: #   #

First Name: #   #

Middle Initial:#   #

Professional Title: #   #

Department/sub-division: #   #

Institution: #   #

Parent Institution: #   #

Street/P.O. box: #   #

City: #   #

Postal code   #   #

Country: #   #

Telephone: #   #

Fax: #   #

Telex: #   #

E-mail :   #   #

ADDITIONAL AFFILIATED INVESTIGATORS:

(Please list in alphabetical order according to last name no more than six. Copy the following 10 lines up to five times to enter information about each person.)

Title: #   #

Last Name: #   #

First Name: #   #

Middle Initial:#   #

Professional Title: #   #

Department/sub-division: #   #

Institution: #   #

Parent Institution: #   #

11.1.2 Survey Questionnaire
Wave II

A Survey of Ageing Research in Europe

Sponsors:

The Population Activities Unit
United Nations Economic Commission for Europe
and
The National Institute on Aging
United States National Institutes of Health

I. GENERAL DESCRIPTION OF THE RESEARCH PROJECT

1. Please repeat the title of the selected research project?

(As indicated in the reference on the invitation letter.)

#   #

2. Please list the names of the investigators in charge of the <u>execution</u> of the project.

(Copy the following lines as many times as necessary. If possible, please restrict the number of investigators to fewer than six. Please enter Mr., Mrs., Miss., or Ms. for a person's title.)

Title:	#	#
Last Name:	#	#
First Name:	#	#
Middle Initial:	#	#
Professional Title:	#	#
Department/sub-division:	#	#
Institution:	#	#
Parent Institution:	#	#

3. Please indicate the name of the contact person of this project

(If the name of the contact person is already listed in question 2, please only give the last and first name of this person below.)

Title:	#	#
Last Name:	#	#
First Name:	#	#
Middle Initial:	#	#
Professional Title:	#	#
Department/sub-division:	#	#
Institution:	#	#
Parent Institution:	#	#
Street/P.O. Box:	#	#
City:	#	#
Postal code:	#	#
Country:	#	#
Telephone:	#	#
Fax:	#	#
Telex:	#	#
E-mail:	#	#

4. What is the state of your project?

(Answer: "planned", "on-going", "finalized", " interrupted")

\#   \#

II. INSTITUTIONAL INFORMATION

> **5. Please provide the name and address of the primary organization in charge of executing this project.**

Institution:	\#	\#
Department/sub-division:	\#	\#
Parent Institution:	\#	\#
Street/P.O. Box:	\#	\#
City:	\#	\#
Postal code:	\#	\#
Country:	\#	\#
Telephone:	\#	\#
Fax:	\#	\#
Telex:	\#	\#
E-mail:	\#	\#

6. Please provide a brief history of this institution.

(Maximum 300 words. Include institution's founding date, notable affiliated scholars, significant contributions to population and ageing research and a description of the institution's research tradition and/or specific comparative advantage.)

\#   \#

7. Are other institutions collaborating on this project?

(Answer: "Yes" or "No")

\#   \#

8. If "Yes", please list the names and addresses of collaborating institutions, as well as the substantive research areas in which they collaborate.

(Copy the following lines as many times as necessary.)

Institution:	\#	\#
Department/sub-division:	\#	\#
Parent Institution:	\#	\#
Substantive research area:	\#	\#
Street/P.O. Box:	\#	\#
City:	\#	\#
Postal code:	\#	\#

Country:	#	#
Telephone:	#	#
Fax:	#	#
Telex:	#	#

9. What organization(s) provides <u>funding</u> for this project?

(Please copy the following lines as many times as necessary.)

Organization:	#	#
Street/P.O. Box:	#	#
City:	#	#
Postal code:	#	#
Country:	#	#

III. BASIC INFORMATION ON THE PROJECT

10. Please describe in detail the most important research questions of the project.

> *(Maximum 500 words. Please refine the broad substantive areas as listed in Wave I.)*

> #   #

11. Please describe briefly the underlying theoretical and methodological approaches of the project.*(Maximum 300 words.)*

> #   #

IV. PROJECT & DATA

12. Please provide a brief general description of the project's study design.

> *(Maximum 300 words.)*

> #   #

13. Please specify the types of data collection and/or analysis activities involved in the project.

> *(Place a "Yes" or "No" next to each of the following categories, as applicable, and specify, if necessary, additional types of activities not mentioned below.)*

Primary survey quantitative data collection and analysis	#	#
Primary survey qualitative data collection and analysis	#	#
Analysis of micro-level census data	#	#
Analysis of micro-level civil register data	#	#
Analysis of micro-level vital statistics	#	#
Analysis of micro-level related administrative data	#	#

        Other (Specify)   #   #

        Other (Specify)   #   #

14. Please list the geographic area(s) included in this project.

    (Specify names of countries, provinces, and/or other relevant sub-national units.)

          #   #

15. What are the units of analyses in this project?

    (Place a "Yes" or "No" next to each of the following categories, as applicable, and, if necessary, specify additional units not mentioned below.)

Individual	#	#
Family	#	#
Household	#	#
Social network	#	#
Neighborhood	#	#
Community	#	#
City	#	#
Province	#	#
Country	#	#
Other (Specify)	#	#
Other (Specify)	#	#

16. Please describe the methods of descriptive analysis employed.

    (Maximum 100 words.)

          #   #

17. Please describe the methods of explanatory analysis employed.

    (Maximum 100 words.)

          #   #

        IF PRIMARY DATA COLLECTION IS NOT PART OF THIS PROJECT, PLEASE GO TO QUESTION 24

18. If primary survey data collection was conducted, please send the survey instrument to the Population Activities Unit, if necessary under separate cover. Please indicate below whether it has been sent. *(Answer "Yes, sent" or "No, not available")*

          #   #

19. If primary survey data collection was conducted, what were:

The sample size	#	#
The sampling proportion(s)	#	#
The response rate	#	#

20. If primary survey data collection was conducted, what were:

     The sampling design   #   #

     The selection criteria   #   #

21. Are these data available (or will they be available) to academic and policy-oriented researchers who are not associated with the project, and if so, under what conditions?

     #   #

22. If these data are (or will be) available, how should an interested researcher apply to obtain access to them?

     #   #

23. Also, if these data are (or will be) available, please send the code book(s), directories or other descriptions of the data to the Population Activities Unit (if necessary under separate cover). Please indicate whether it has been sent.

(Answer: "Yes, sent" or" No, not available")

     #   #

V. RESULTS AND PUBLICATIONS

24. Please describe, if appropriate, the (preliminary) results of this project.
(Maximum 300 words.)

     #   #

25. Please list the most important reports and publications resulting from this project.
(Copy the following lines as many times as necessary. If possible however, list fewer than six reports or publications and send a separate bibliography if there is a more extensive list available.)

Author(s) / Editor(s):   #   #
Year of publication: #   #
Title: #   #
Publisher: #   #
Place: #   #

26. Please send to the Population Activities Unit copies of the most important published research articles and reports based on this project, if they are available. Please indicate the number of articles and reports being sent.
(Answer: "Yes" and the number of articles being sent, or" No, not available")

     #   #

VI. FUTURE AGEING RESEARCH IN EUROPE

27. Please briefly describe future plans (the next 5 to 7 years) for conducting ageing-related research at the primary organization in charge of executing this project.

(Maximum 150 words.)

#   #

28. Please list up to six European surveys or other data collection and research efforts of particular importance to ageing related research in the next decade.

(Copy the following lines as many times as necessary. Please restrict the number of such efforts to fewer than six.)

Name of Survey or Data Collection and Research Effort: #   #
Executing Institution: #   #
Status (Answer: "planned", "on-going" or "finalized") :   #   #

29. Where, in your view, should ageing research in Europe focus in the next ten years?

(Maximum 300 words.)

#   #

30. In your view, would it be desirable to create a new pan-European survey that would support cross-national comparative research on issues related to various aspects of population ageing and the status of the older population?

(If no, state "No" and, if you wish, provide justification; if yes, indicate what should be the objectives of such a survey. Maximum 300 words.)

#   #

RESPONDENT'S PERSONAL INFORMATION:

Title:	#	#
Last Name:	#	#
First Name:	#	#
Middle Initial:	#	#
Professional Title:	#	#
Department/Sub-division:	#	#
Institution:	#	#
Parent-Institution:	#	#
Street/P.O. Box:	#	#
City:	#	#
Postal code	#	#
Country:	#	#
Telephone:	#	#
Fax:	#	#
Telex:	#	#
E-mail :	#	#

11.3. PROJECTS BY COUNTRY

AUSTRIA

7.2.11 Population ageing and inter-generational equity in pension systems

BELGIUM

7.3.8   Elderly women in Europe: Choices and challenges

BULGARIA

7.1.9   Restriction in daily living activity among elderly

DENMARK

7.1.4 Oldest-Old mortality: Demographic models and analyses
7.1.24 The development in health expectancy in Denmark
7.3.5   The vulnerable elderly and elder politics

FINLAND

7.1.2   European longitudinal study on aging (ELSA)
7.1.17 Ageing in an epidemiological-ecological context (NORA)
7.2.10 Work and retirement among older workers In Finland
7.3.10 Adult education for the elderly in Scandinavia
7.4.3   Use of open and institutional care policies for the dependent elderly

FRANCE

7.1.14 PAQUID study of normal and pathological aging
7.2.9   Life course of 2 cohorts of retirees of the Greater Paris
7.3.4   Relations between generations and family support to elderly people

GERMANY

7.2.7   The German socio-economic panel (GSOEP) English language public use files
7.3.2   German aging survey
7.5.1   Berlin aging study (BASE)
7.5.2   German interdisciplinary longitudinal study on adulthood and aging (ILSE)
7.4.4   Acceptance and benefits of extended in-home services for rural elderly needing care

HUNGARY

7.1.25 Biological, clinical, morphological and personality parameters of longevity
7.6.4   Survey of people 70 years or over
7.6.5   Survey on persons aged 50 or over (born in 1944 or earlier)

ICELAND

7.1.23 Reykjavik 80+: A longitudinal study of 80 year-olds and older in Iceland

ISRAEL

7.1.7   The elderly aged 60 and over in households in Israel
7.1.10 The cross-sectional and longitudinal aging study (CALAS)

ITALY

7.1.5   Italian longitudinal study on aging (ILSA)
7.1.18 Changes in elderly mortality and projections of the elderly population
7.1.26 I CARe Dicomano: Cardiac failure in the elderly residents in Dicomano

LATVIA

7.6.6   Living conditions survey in Latvia

LUXEMBOURG

7.2.3   Luxembourg income study

THE NETHERLANDS

7.1.1   Longitudinal aging study Amsterdam
7.1.3   Gröningen longitudinal aging study (GLAS) on functional status and need for care
7.1.6   Amsterdam study on the elderly (AMSTEL)
7.1.20 SENECA
7.1.21 EUGERON
7.2.1   Economic aspects of aging
7.2.4   Dutch socio-economic panel study (DSEP)
7.2.5   The VSB savings project
7.2.6   Savings and pensions: Structural analysis of household savings and wealth
7.3.1   Living arrangements and social networks of older adults

NORWAY

7.3.6   Teenagers reach retirement age: A longitudinal study

RUSSIA

7.6.3   The Russia longitudinal monitoring survey (RLMS)

SPAIN

7.1.12 Aging in Leganés
7.4.1   Informal support for the elderly (Part I and II)

SWEDEN

7.1.8   The Swedish adoption/twin study of ageing (SATSA)
7.1.11 The Swedish panel study of living conditions of the oldest old (SWEOLD)
7.1.22 Lund 80+. A longitudinal, sequential study of 80 year-olds and older
7.3.9   Daily life among the old-old and the oldest-old: A Nordic comparative study

SWITZERLAND

7.2.12 Transitions to retirement
7.5.3   The autonomy of the aging population in Switzerland

UNITED KINGDOM

7.1.15 Nottingham longitudinal study of activity and ageing (NLSAA)
7.1.16 Melton Mowbray ageing project
7.2.2   OPCS retirement surveys
7.2.8   International retirement migration of Britons to southern Europe (1994-97)

11.4 Contact Addresses by Project

7.1.1 Longitudinal aging study Amsterdam
Dr. Dorly J. H. Deeg
Longitudinal Aging StudyAmsterdam
Vrije Universiteit
De Boelelaan 1081c
Amsterdam, 1081 HV The Netherlands
Tel: (+31) - 20 - 444 6770
Fax: (+31) - 20 - 444 6775
E-Mail: Dorly_Deeg@sara.nl

7.1.10 The cross-sectional and longitudinal aging study (CALAS)
Prof. Baruch Modan
Clinical Epidemioloy
Chaim Sheba Medical Center
Tel Hashomer, 52621 Israel
Tel: (+972) -3-5303261
Fax: (+972) -3-5348360
E-Mail: epid03@ccsg.tau.ac.il

7.1.11 The Swedish panel study of living conditions of the oldest old (SWEOLD)
Mr. Mats Thorslund
Dept. of Social Work
Stockholm University
Stockholm S-106 91 Sweden
Tel: (+46) -8-16 21 06
Fax: (+46) - 8-16 57 96
E-Mail: Mats.Thorslund@social.su.se

7.1.12 Aging in Leganés
Ms. María-Victoria Zunzunegui
Epidemiology
Escuela Andaluza de Salud Pública
Apartado Correos 2070
Granada, 18080 Spain
Tel: (+34) -58-161044
Fax: (+34) -58-161142
E-Mail: 100433.2527@compuserve.com

7.1.13 National-ethnic peculiarities of aging in Ukraine
Dr. Svetlana Michailovna Kuznetsova
Rehabilitation Centre
Institute of Gerontology
Academy of Medical Science
Vyshgorodskaya str. 67
Kiev, 252114 Ukraine
Tel: (+7) 44 4300537

7.1.14 PAQUID. Study of normal and pathological aging

Jean Francois Dartigues
INSERM U 330
Université de Bordeaux II
146 rue Leo Saignat
F-33076 Bordeaux France

7.1.15 Nottingham longitudinal study of activity and ageing (NLSAA)

Dr. Kevin Morgan
Senior Lecturer
Departments of Health Care of the Elderly and Physiology and Pharmacology
Queen's Medical Centre, University of Nottingham
Clifton Boulevard
Nottingham, NG7 2UH United Kingdom
Tel: (+44) - 114 -271 4645
Fax: (+44) - 114 -256 0472

7.1.16 Melton Mowbray ageing project

Dr. Carol Jagger
Epidemiology and Public Health
University of Leicester
22-28 Princess Road West
Leicester, LE1 6TP United Kingdom
Tel: (+44) - 0116 - 523156
Fax: (+44) - 0116 - 523272
E-Mail: cxj@le.ac.uk

7.1.17 Ageing in an epidemiological-ecological context. A five-year follow-up study of 75-year-old people living in three Nordic localities (NORA)

Mr. Eino M. Heikkinen
The Finnish Centre for Interdisciplinary Gerontology
University of Jyväskylä
P.O. Box 35
Jyväskylä FIN-40351 Finland
Tel: (+358) 41 602 166
Fax: (+358) 41 602 011
E-Mail: Heikkine@maila.jyu.fi

7.1.18 Changes in elderly mortality and projections of the elderly population

Mr. Frank Heins
Institute of Population Research
National Research Council
Viale Beethoven, 56
Roma 00144 Italy
Tel: (+39) - 06-5925248
Fax: (+39) - 06-5925414
E-Mail: A04300@IRMRETI.CED.RM.CNR.IT

7.1.19 Alternative population projections for major world regions
Mr. Wolfgang Lutz
International Institute for Applied Systems Analysis (IIASA)
Schlossplatz 1
A-2361 Laxenburg Austria
Tel: (+43) - 2236-807
Fax: (+43) - 2236-71313
E-Mail: lutz@iiasa.ac.at

7.1.19 Biological, clinical, morphological and personality parameters of longevity
Director, Prof. Dr. Iván László
Clinical Gerontology Center
Semmelweis University of Medicine
Rökk Szilárd utca 13. POB 45.H.1428
Budapest, 1085 Hungary
Tel: (+ 361) - 113-5411
Fax: (+ 361) - 210-0329
E-Mail: ivanlas@geront sote hu

7.1.2 European longitudinal study on aging
Mr. Eino Heikkinen
Department of Health Sciences
The Finnish Centre of Interdiciplinary Gerontology
University of Jyväskylä
P.O.Box 35
Jyväskylä, FIN-40351 Finland
Tel: (+358) 41 602 160
Fax: (+358) 41 602 011
E-Mail: heikkine@maila.jyu.fi

7.1.20 SENECA
Dr. Lisette C. P. G. M. de Groot
Dept. of Human Nutrition
Wageningen Agricultural University
Bomenweg 2
Wageningen, 6703 HD the Netherlands
Tel: (+ 31) - 317 - 482589
Fax: (+ 31) - 317 - 483342

7.1.21 EUGERON
Dr. Johannes J. F. Schroots
Director, Faculty of Psychology
ERGO/European Research Institute on Health & Aging
University of Amsterdam
Roetersstraat 15
Amsterdam 1018 WB The Netherlands
Tel: (+ 31) -20-5256830
Fax: (+ 31) -20-6390279
E-Mail: op_Schroots@macmail.psy.uva.nl

7.1.22 Lund 80+. A longitudinal, sequential study of 80 year-olds and older

Dr. Torbjörn Svensson
Gerontology Research Center
Karl XII-g 1
Lund S-22220 Sweden
Tel: (+46) - 46 131948
Fax: (+46) - 46 130940
E-Mail: geron@gemini.ldc.lu.se

7.1.24 The development in health expectancy in Denmark

Dr. Henrik Brønnum-Hansen
The Danish Institute for Clinical Epidemiology
Ministry of Health
25, Svanemøllevej
Copenhagen Ø, DK-2100 Denmark
Tel: (+45) 31 20 77 77
Fax: (+45) 31 20 80 10

7.1.26 I CARe Dicomano: Cardiac failure in the elderly residents in Dicomano

Mr. Mauro Di Bari
Department of Gerontology and Geriatric Medicine
University of Florence
via delle Oblate, 4
Florence, 50141 ITALY
Tel: (+39) -55-410766 or 55-5277579
Fax: (+39)-55-4223879
E-Mail: GER1@CESIT1.UNIFI.IT

7.1.3 Groningen longitudinal aging study (GLAS) on functional status and need for care

Dr. G. I. J. M. Kempen
School of Medicine, University of Groningen
Northern Center for Health Care Research
A. Deusinglaan 1
Groningen, 9713 AV The Netherlands
Tel: (+31) 50 3633208/3633065
Fax: (+31) 50 3632406
E-Mail: G.K.J.M.Kempen@med.rug.nl

7.1.5 Italian longitudinal study on aging (ILSA)

Dr. Stefania Maggi
Target Project on Aging
National Research Council (CNR)
Via Tiburtina, 770
ROMA, 00159 ITALY
Tel: (+39) 6 4075891
Fax: (+39) 6 4075827
E-Mail: MC5516@MCLINK.IT

7.1.6 Amsterdam study on the elderly (AMSTEL)

Mr. Cees Jonker
Psychiatry of Elderly People and the Institute for Research in Extramural Medicine
Vrije Universiteit, Amsterdam
Prins Hendriklaan 29
Amsterdam 1075 AZ The Netherlands
Tel: (+31) -20 673 3535
Fax: (+31) -20 662 3677

7.1.7 The elderly aged 60 and over in households in Israel

Ms. Dorith Tal
Head of Population Section
Demography, Population, & Immigrant Absorption
Central Bureau of Statistics
P.O. Box 13015
Jerusalem, 91130 Israel
Tel: (+972) 2-655-33-75
Fax: (+972) 2-655-33-92

7.1.9 Restriction in daily living activity among elderly

Mrs. Margareta N. Mutafova
Assist. Professor
Social Medicine and Public Health
Medical University
Ministry of Health
8 Belo More
Sofia, 1504 Bulgaria
Tel: (+359) -2 44 23 88
Fax: (+359) -2 44 23 88

7.2.1 Economic aspects of aging

Mr. Maarten Lindeboom
Dept of Economics
Leiden University
P.O.Box 9521
Leiden, 2300 RA The Netherlands
Tel: (+31) -071-5277855
Fax: (+31) -071-5277732
E-Mail: jfaekh@ruljur.leidenuniv.nl
or jfaejt@ruljur.leidenuniv.nl

7.2.11 Population ageing and inter-generational equity in pension systems

Dr. Christopher Prinz
Social Welfare Modelling Programme
European Centre for Social Welfare Policy and Research
Berggasse 17
Vienna A-1090 Austria
Tel: (+43) -1- 3194505-32
Fax: (+43) - 1- 3194505-19
E-Mail: x0261daa@vm.univie.ac.at

7.2.12 Transitions to retirement

Dr. Hans-Dieter Schneider
Department of Psychology
Gerontological Research Group
University of Fribourg
Rue Faucigny 2
Fribourg, CH-1701 Switzerland
Tel: (+41) -37-297-672
Fax: (+41) 1-37-299-712
E-Mail: Regula.Buchmueller@unifr.ch

7.2.2 Analyses of OPCS retirement surveys

Ms. Rebecca Goldman
Senior Research Officer
Personal Sector Research
Institute for Fiscal Studies
7 Ridgmount Street
London, WC1E 7AE United Kingdom
Tel: (+44) - 0171-636 3784
Fax: (+44) - 0171-323 4780
E-Mail: goldmanr@asdmain.asd-dss.gov.uk

7.2.3 Luxembourg income study

Ms. Inge O'Connor
Administrative Assistant, United States Office
Luxembourg Income Study
426 Eggers Hall
Syracuse University
Syracuse, New York, 13244-1090 United States of America
Tel: (+001) -315-443-9042
Fax: (+001) -315-443-1081
E-Mail: tmsmeeding@maxwell.syr.edu

7.2.7 The English language public use file of the German socio-economic panel

Ms. Elke Holst
Center for Policy Research
Syracuse University
426 Eggers Hall
Syracuse, NY, 13244-1090 United States of America
Tel: (+001) -315-443-9040
Fax: (+001) -315-443-1081
E-Mail: burk@maxwell.syr.edu

7.2.8 International retirement migration of Britons to Southern Europe (1994-97)

Prof. Anthony Warnes
Dept. of Health Care for Elderly People
University of Sheffield Northern General Hospital
Herries Road
Sheffield, S5 7AU United Kingdom
Tel: (+44) - 0114 271 5773
Fax: (+44) -0114 271 5771
E-Mail: A.WARNES@SHEFFIELD.A.C.UK

7.2.9 Life course of two cohorts of retirees of the Greater Paris

Dr. Françoise Cribier (Mrs)
équipe de géographie sociale et gérontologie
CNRS-University Paris 7
191 rue Saint-Jacques
Paris, 75 005 France
Tel: (+33) 1 46 34 51 96
Fax: (+33) 1 43 25 25 89

7.3.1 Living arrangements & social networks of older adults

Prof. Cees Knipscheer
Dept. of Sociology and Social Gerontology
Faculty of Social and Cultural Sciences
de Boelelaan 1081 C
Amsterdam, 1081 HV The Netherlands
Tel: (+ 31) -20-444 6800
Fax: (+ 31) -20-444 6810

7.3.10 Adult education for the elderly in Scandinavia

Dr. Jan-Erik Ruth
Kuntokallio Center for Gerontological Training and Research
Kuntokallio Rd 1.
Östersundom, 01100 Finland
Tel: (+358) - 877 9383
Fax: (+358) - 8779981

7.3.2 German aging survey

Dr. Harald Künemund
Forschungsgruppe Altern und Lebenslauf (FALL)
Freie Universität Berlin
Babelsberger Str. 14-16
Berlin, 10715 Germany
Tel: (+49) 30 85002 210
Fax: (+49) 30 85002 205
E-Mail: sekretar@zedat.fu-berlin.de

7.3.3 Bangor longitudinal study of ageing

Prof. G. Clare Wenger
Centre for Social Policy Research,
School of Sociology and Social Policy
University of Wales
Bangor, LL57 2DG United Kingdom
Tel: (+44) - 01248 382230
Fax: (+44)- 01248 362029
E-Mail: g.c.wenger@bangor.ac.

7.3.4 Relations between generations and family support to elderly people

Ms. Claudine Attias-Donfut
Research Department on Ageing,
Caisse Nationale d'Assurance Vieillesse
49 rue Mirabeau
Paris, 75016 France
Tel: (+33) - 1 45 27 78 24
Fax: (+33) - 1 45 25 89 64

7.3.5 The vulnerable elderly and elder politics

Mr. Eigil B Hansen
AKF, Institute of Local Government Studies.
Nyropsgade 37
Copenhagen V, DK-1602 Denmark
Tel: (+ 45) 33 11 03 00
Fax: (+ 45) 33 15 28 75
E-Mail: akf@akf.dk

7.3.6 Teenagers reach retirement age: a longitudinal study

Mr. Sol Seim
Emeritus Researcher
Norwegian Institute of Gerontology
Oscarsgt. 36
Oslo, 0258 Norway
Tel: (+47) 22 55 7420
Fax: (+47) 22 56 1950
E-Mail: Susan.Lingsom@isaf.no

7.3.7 Women as they age: a challenge
7.3.8 Elderly women in Europe: Choices and challenges

Mr. Gilbert H. Dooghe
Ministry of the Flemish Community-CBGS
Markiesstraat 1
Brussels, 1000 Belgium
Tel: 02 - 507 35 68
Fax: 02 -507 35 57

7.3.9 Daily life among the old-old and the oldest-old: A Nordic comparative study

Mr. Lars Andersson
Head of Research, Associate Professor
Social Gerontology
Stockholm Gerontology Research Center
Box 6401
Stockholm, S-113 82 Sweden
Tel: (+46) 8 6905807
Fax: (+46) 8 335275
E-Mail: Lars Andersson@knv.ki.se

7.4.1 Informal support for the elderly

Mr. Manuel Justel
Centro de Investigaciones Sociológicas
Ministerio de la Presidencia
Montalbán,8
Madrid, 28014 Spain
Tel: -(+34) 91 5 80 76 02
Fax: -(+34) 91 5 80 76 19

7.4.2 Transport for elderly persons: Mobility survey of ten counties in England & Wales

Dr. Francis Jegede
Geography Department
University of Derby
Kedleston Road
Derby, DE22 1GB United Kingdom
Tel: (+ 44) -1332-622222 Ext. 1737
Fax: (+44) -1332-622747
E-Mail: F.J.Jegede@derby.ac.uk

7.4.3 Use of open and institutional care policies for the dependent elderly

Dr. Anja Noro
Health Services Research Unit
National Research and Development Centre for Welfare and Health (Stakes)
P.O. Box 220
Helsinki, Fin-00531 Finland
Tel: (+ 358) 0 39671
Fax: (+ 358) 0 3967 2485
E-Mail: anja.noro@stakes.fi

7.4.4 Acceptance and benefits of extended in-home services for rural elderly needing care

Ms. Leonore Link
Interdisciplinary Research Group for Applied Social Gerontology
University of Kassel
Mönchebergstr. 19b
Kassel, D-34109 Germany
Tel: (+49) - 0561804-2478
Fax: (+49) - 0561 804-3283

7.5.1 Berlin aging study (BASE)

Mr. Reinhard V. Nuthmann
Committee on Aging and Societal Development
Berlin-Brandenburg Academy of Sciences
Jaegerstr. 22/23
Berlin, 10117 Germany
Tel: (+49) - 30 203 70 -620/-562
Fax: (+49) - 30 203 70 -500/-214

7.5.2 German interdisciplinary longitudinal study on adulthood and aging (ILSE)

Dr., Mrs. Elisabeth M. Minnemann
Institute of Gerontology
University of Heidelberg
Bergheimer Straße 20
Heidelberg, 69115 Germany
Tel: (+49) -6221-548181
Fax: (+49) -6221-545961
E-Mail: gero@urz.uni-heidelberg.de

7.5.3 The autonomy of the aging population in Switzerland

Mrs. Astrid K. Stuckelberger
Teaching and research coordinator,
Centre for Interdisciplinary Gerontology (CIG)
University of Geneva
59, route de Mon-Idée
Thônex-Geneva, CH-1226 Switzerland
Tel: (+41) -22-305 66 01
Fax: (+41) -22-348 90 77
E-Mail: cig@ibm.unige.ch

7.6.1 Dynamics of population ageing in ECE countries

Mr. Miroslav Macura
Chief, Population Activities Unit
Economic Commission for Europe
Palais des Nations
CH-1211 Geneva 10 Switzerland
Tel: (+41) 22-917-2760
Fax: (+41) 22-917-0101
E-Mail: Miroslav.Macura@UNECE.ORG

7.6.3 The Russia longitudinal monitoring survey (RLMS)

Dr. Namvar Zohoori
Carolina Population Center
University of North Carolina at Chapel Hill
CB 8120, University Square East
Chapel Hill, NC 27516 United States of America
Tel: (+001) -919-966-2157
Fax: (+001) -919-966-6638
E-Mail: NAMVAR_ZOHOORI@UNC.EDU

7.6.4 Survey of people 70 years or over

Councillor. Ms. Gabriella Vukovich
Head of department
Population census department
Hungarian Central Statistical Office
Petrezselyem 7-9
Budapest II 1024 Hungary
Tel: (+36) -1 212-6569
Fax: (+36) -1 212-6679

7.6.5 Survey on persons aged 50 or over (born in 1944 or earlier)

Mr. Árpád Mészáros
Population Census Department
Hungarian Central Statistical Office
Petrezselyem 7-9
Budapest II. 1024 Hungary
Tel: - (+36) -1 212-6569
Fax: (+36) -1 212-6679

7.6.6 Living conditions survey in Latvia
Dr. Aadne Aasland
FAFO, Institute for Applied Social Science
Borggata 2B, P.O Box 2947 Tøyen
Oslo, N-0608 NORWAY
Tel: (+47) -22 67 60 00
Fax: (+47) -22 67 60 22